The IDEA MAGAZINE FOR TEACHERS®

MAILBOX®

The Education Center®

2008–2009 YEARBOOK

The Education Center, Inc.
Greensboro, North Carolina

The Mailbox® 2008–2009 Kindergarten Yearbook

Managing Editor, *The Mailbox* Magazine: Sharon M. Tresino

Editorial Team: Becky S. Andrews, Diane Badden, Kimberley Bruck, Karen A. Brudnak, Kimberly Brugger-Murphy, Pam Crane, Lynn Drolet, Amy Erickson, Sarah Foreman, Pierce Foster, Margaret Freed (COVER ARTIST), Tazmen Hansen, Marsha Heim, Lori Z. Henry, Krystle Short Jones, Debra Liverman, Kitty Lowrance, Jennifer Nunn, Tina Petersen, Mark Rainey, Greg D. Rieves, Kelly Robertson, Hope Rodgers, Eliseo De Jesus Santos II, Rebecca Saunders, Hope Taylor Spencer, Donna K. Teal, Rachael Traylor, Zane Williard

ISBN10 1-56234-921-X
ISBN13 978-156234-921-9
ISSN 1088-5552

Printed in the United States of America.

The Education Center, Inc.
P.O. Box 9753
Greensboro, NC 27429-0753

Look for *The Mailbox® 2009–2010 Kindergarten Yearbook* in the summer of 2010. The Education Center, Inc., is the publisher of *The Mailbox®*, *Teacher's Helper®*, and *Learning®* magazines, as well as other fine products. Look for these wherever quality teacher materials are sold, call 1-800-714-7991, or visit www.themailbox.com.

Contents

Math Units

Seasonal Units

Index

Arts & Crafts

Arts & Crafts

Student Look-Alikes

These projects are so cute, you'll want to show them off! Display them with students' names or photos during open house.

Materials for one project:
oval template (face)
skin-toned sheet of paper
lengths of yarn (hair)
kidney beans (eyebrows and hair)
pasta twists (hair)
scissors
crayons
glue

Steps:
1. Trace the oval on the paper. Cut out the tracing.
2. To make a self-likeness, draw your face on the cutout. Then glue yarn, kidney beans, and/or pasta twists to the cutout to add hair and any other desired details.

Sheila Criqui-Kelley, Lebo Elementary, Lebo, KS

Apple and Friend

For easy lacing, dip a few inches of one yarn end in white glue and then allow it to dry. The result will be a sturdy lacing tip that doesn't fray!

Materials for one apple project:
2 large identical apple cutouts with holes punched along the edges
piece of tissue paper
green construction paper scraps
3" brown pipe cleaner
length of yarn
4 small green pom-poms
scissors
glue
tape
black marker

Steps:
1. Fold a piece of green paper in half. Draw a leaf on the fold as shown. Cut it out.
2. Unfold the leaf, place the pipe cleaner on the crease, and then glue the leaf closed. Tape the pipe cleaner to one apple to make a stem.
3. Begin lacing the two apples together with yarn so the taped end of the pipe cleaner is on the inside. When the apples are almost entirely laced, gently stuff them with crumpled tissue paper. Then finish lacing the apples.
4. Glue the pom-poms on the apple to make a worm. Draw two eyes on the worm.

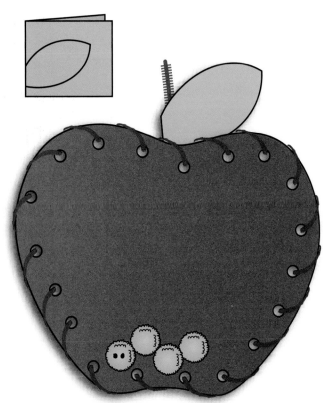

Amy Melisi, Peaslee Elementary, Northboro, MA

Quick and Easy Owl

No patterns are needed for this project!

Materials for one owl:
6" x 9" brown construction paper
two 3" x 6" brown construction paper rectangles
yellow, black, and orange construction paper scraps
white and brown paint in shallow containers
scissors
glue

Steps:
1. Vertically position the 6" x 9" paper. Cut off the two bottom corners as shown.
2. Cut two eyes, two pupils, and a beak from paper scraps. Glue them in place.
3. Cut a wing from each 3" x 6" rectangle. Fringe-cut the straight edge of each wing. Glue the wings to the back of the owl.
4. Cut two triangles (feet) from paper scraps. Glue them in place.
5. Use the paint to make fingerprints on the owl's body.

Sweet Sheep

This adorable idea is perfect to use with a farm unit or *Russell the Sheep* by Rob Scotton.

Materials for one sheep:
1½" x 2" gray construction paper oval
gray construction paper scraps
2 wooden clothespins
cotton balls
craft stick
black marker
scissors
glue

Steps:
1. Draw hooves on the clothespins as shown.
2. Clip the clothespins to the craft stick to make the project self-standing.
3. Draw a sheep face on the gray oval. Cut two ears from gray paper scraps and then glue them to the oval. Glue the oval to one end of the craft stick.
4. Stretch out cotton balls. Glue them to the sheep's head and body.

Heather Moseley, Carver Kindergarten, Lockhart, TX

Arts & Crafts

Speedy Fire Truck

This project is a perfect token of appreciation for your local firefighters!

Materials for one truck:
4½" x 10" red construction paper rectangle with a slit in one
    long side as shown
white and black construction paper scraps
length of yarn
scissors
glue

Steps:
1. Cut a window and two wheels from black paper. Glue them in place.
2. Cut two long strips and several short strips from white paper. Glue them on the truck to make a ladder.
3. Squeeze some glue on the truck where you want the hose to be. Then arrange the yarn to make the hose.

Cute Cat

Sticky dots make it simple for students to make the eyes on this adorable feline.

Materials for one cat:
2 black circles, one 6" and one 8"
black construction paper scraps
black pipe cleaner
2 green sticky dots
pom-pom
orange yarn cut into short lengths

yarn or ribbon bow
masking tape
glue
black marker
white crayon

Steps:
1. Fold the pipe cleaner in half and twist it to make a tail. Tape the ends of the pipe cleaner to the eight-inch circle. Place the circle taped-side down.
2. Glue the six-inch circle to the eight-inch circle as shown.
3. Cut two ears from black paper. Glue them in place.
4. Put the two sticky dots on the head to make eyes. Draw black pupils.
5. Glue the pom-pom to the head to make the nose. Glue lengths of orange yarn to the cat to make whiskers. Draw a mouth with the white crayon.
6. Glue the bow below the head.

adapted from an idea by Beth Dillie
Markesan Elementary
Markesan, WI

Pumpkin Puzzle

Since each of these pumpkins is unique, this idea is great to pair with a discussion about individuality and *The Legend of Spookley the Square Pumpkin* by Joe Troiano.

Materials for one pumpkin:
pumpkin cutout without a stem
black sheet of paper
green and yellow construction paper scraps
scissors
glue
ruler (optional)
pencil (optional)

Steps:
1. Cut the pumpkin into several vertical strips and then reassemble it on the black paper. (For an easier version, use a ruler and a pencil to divide the pumpkin into several vertical sections. Lightly number the sections before you cut them apart.) Glue the strips to the paper, leaving space between them.
2. Cut a stem from green paper. Glue it in place.
3. Cut facial features from yellow paper. Then glue them to the pumpkin.

Sarah Bajema
White Pine Academy
Lansing, MI

Fingerprint Gobbler

Set out wet wipes to make it easy for children to clean their fingers between rows of prints.

Materials for one turkey:
paper labeled with four arcs, like the one shown
white paper
paint in the following colors: brown, orange, yellow, and red
black marker
scissors

Steps:
1. Place the blank paper atop the paper with the arcs.
2. Using the paper with the arcs as a placement guide, make a thumbprint (turkey body) with brown paint as shown. Then make fingerprints in four arcs around the turkey's body, using a different color of paint for each arc. Allow the paint to dry.
3. Draw two eyes, a beak, and two legs. Then trim the paper as desired.

Kelly Kramer
Rivercrest Elementary
Bartlett, TN

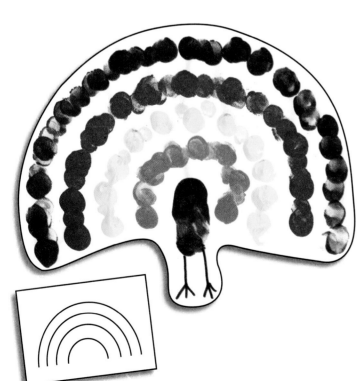

Arts & Crafts

Blushing Santa

Materials for one Santa:
9" x 12" white construction paper
9" x 12" red construction paper
construction paper scraps
pink blush
cotton balls
scissors
glue

Steps:
1. To make a head, round the corners of the white paper.
2. Cut facial details from paper scraps and glue them to the face.
3. Use a cotton ball to rub blush on the cheeks.
4. Cut a hat from the red paper and glue it to the head.
5. Stretch out a few cotton balls and glue them to the hat and face as shown.

Nancy Hayes
Victor Haen School
Kaukauna, WI

Sassy Snowpal

Materials for one snowpal:
blue construction paper
white paper circles: 1 small, 1 large
golf ball
spoon
shallow empty container
shallow container of white paint
craft supplies such as fabric scraps, sequins, rick-rack, paper scraps, yarn
glue
scissors

Steps:
1. Place the blue paper in the empty container.
2. Use the spoon to dip the golf ball in the paint and then place the ball on the paper.
3. Tilt the container back and forth to roll the ball over the paper.
4. After the paint is dry, glue the circles to the paper.
5. Use the craft supplies to add details to the snowpal.

Judith Wrenick
Fraser Valley Elementary
Fraser, CO

Oh, Christmas Tree!

Materials for one tree ornament:
six 1" rings cut from a cardboard tube
construction paper scraps
mini pom-poms
ribbon
green paint
paintbrush
scissors
glue

Steps:
1. Paint the inside and outside of the rings green.
2. When the paint is dry, glue the rings together to make a tree.
3. Glue pom-poms (ornaments) and other desired details to the tree.
4 Tie a length of ribbon to the tree for a hanger.

Suzanne Ward
Caledonia Centennial Public School
Caledonia, Ontario, Canada

A Handy Reindeer

Materials for one reindeer:
9" x 12" tan construction paper
white paper plate
red pom-pom
sticky dots
brown paint
paintbrush
glue
markers

Steps:
1. Paint the plate brown and allow it to dry.
2. Trace both your hands on the tan paper.
3. Cut out the tracings and glue them to the plate so they look like antlers.
4 Add sticky-dot eyes and a pom-pom nose.
5. Draw a mouth.

Amy Rodriguez
Public School 212
Brooklyn, NY

Arts & Crafts

Monkey Business

No patterns are required to make these adorable valentine holders!

Materials for one valentine holder:
5 circles: 2 matching red, 1 slightly smaller pink (face), and
    2 matching smaller pink (ears)
sentence strip
hole puncher
yarn
glue
crayons
stapler

Steps:
1. Glue the face and ears to one red circle and make a few rips at the top of the red circle to create tufts of hair.
2. Use a crayon to add ear and facial details.
3. Stack the red circles and staple the lower edges together from ear to ear.
4. Staple a personalized sentence strip to the bottom of the project.
5. Just above each ear, punch a hole through both red circles and attach a yarn handle.

Fishy Fanfare

Plan to complete this project over two days to allow time for the paint to dry.

Materials for one fish:
12" x 18" white construction paper
paint
pom-pom
scissors
glue
marker

Steps:
1. Fold the paper in half; then open it and drizzle paint on one half.
2. Refold the paper and smooth it with your hands; then reopen it.
3. After the paint is dry, refold the paper. Along the fold, cut out three different-size heart halves.
4. Unfold the cutouts and cut the smallest one in half. Glue the hearts together as shown.
5. Glue on the pom-pom for an eye. Then add desired details with the marker.

Lovely Lion

Make these projects at the beginning of March to remind students that March comes roaring in like a lion.

Materials for one lion:
circles: large brown (mane) and smaller tan (face)
round oat cereal pieces
black or brown pom-pom
scissors
glue
crayons

Steps:
1. Fringe-cut the mane.
2. Glue the face to the mane.
3. Glue cereal pieces on the mane.
4. Glue the pom-pom to the face to make a nose. Then use the crayons to add other desired details.

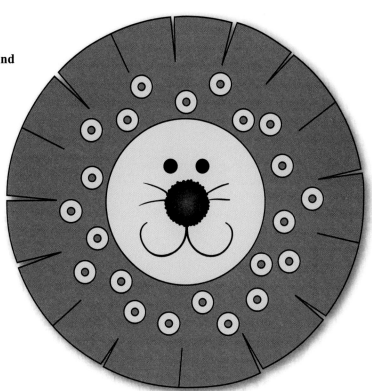

Shiny Shamrock

In honor of St. Patrick's Day, make a shamrock garden by placing the projects in blocks of green craft foam.

Materials for one shamrock:
three 6" paper plates
jumbo craft stick
green paint
gold glitter
glue
masking tape

Steps:
1. Paint the plates and the craft stick.
2. Sprinkle gold glitter on the wet paint.
3. After the paint is dry, glue the plates together so they look like a shamrock.
4. Tape the craft stick to the back of the plates so it looks like a stem.

Amy Rodriguez
Public School 212
Brooklyn, NY

Arts & Crafts

Butterfly Buddy

When a student takes home this eye-catching project, she can use it to display her favorite schoolwork on her refrigerator.

Materials for one butterfly:
tagboard copy of a butterfly pattern from page 17
5" square of clear transparency
spring-type clothespin
magnetic tape
permanent markers
scissors

Steps:
1. Trace the butterfly onto the transparency with a permanent marker.
2. Use the markers to color the butterfly.
3. Cut out the butterfly. Then glue it to the clothespin, making sure the closed part is at the bottom.
4. After the glue dries, adhere a strip of magnetic tape to the clothespin as shown.

Cheryl Bowne
Austin Christian Academy
Austin, TX

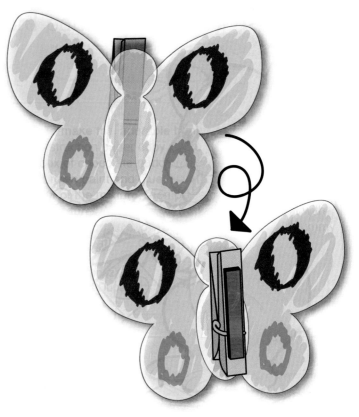

Happy Mother's Day!

Invite each youngster to present this gift to his loved one on Mother's Day.

Materials for one gift:
copy of a message card from page 17
9" x 12" construction paper
paint
marker
crayons
glue

Steps:
1. Make a footprint with paint near the bottom right corner of the vertical paper.
2. When the paint is dry, use a marker to draw a vase shape around your footprint.
3. Draw flowers in the vase.
4. Color the message card and glue it on the paper. Then write your name on the paper.

Diane Bonica
Deer Creek Elementary
Tigard, OR

I love you from my head to my toes!

Love, Harrison

A Colorful Fish

Have students make these eye-catching projects as a follow-up to a reading of *The Rainbow Fish* by Marcus Pfister.

Materials for one fish:
colorful crepe paper streamers
resealable plastic bag
2 sticky dots
scissors
marker
stapler

Steps:

1. Stuff crepe paper streamers in the bag; then seal the bag.
2. To make a mouth, cut a small notch at the bottom of the bag as shown.
3. Attach a sticky dot (eye) to each side of the bag and use the marker to add pupils.
4. Staple a few streamers to the opposite end of the bag so they resemble a tail.

Jennifer Cory, Lingerfeldt Elementary, Gastonia, NC

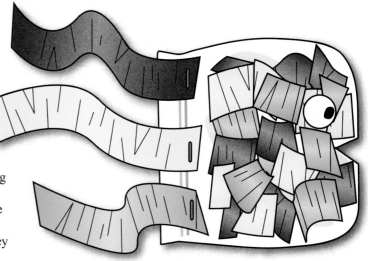

Graduation Buddy

Display these self-portraits to commemorate kindergarten graduation or to celebrate the end of the school year.

Materials for one buddy:
tagboard tracers of the cap patterns on page 18
9" x 12" construction paper
paper strips: 2" x 6", 1" x 4½"
construction paper scraps
9" white paper plate
paint to match skin tone
paintbrush
glue
scissors

Steps:

1. Paint the plate.
2. When the paint is dry, use the paper scraps to make the plate look like your face.
3. Trace the cap patterns on construction paper and cut out the tracings. Glue them to the plate as shown.
4. To make the tassel, fringe-cut the 2" x 6" strip and roll it around a pencil; then glue the end in place before removing the pencil.
5. Glue one end of the 1" x 4½" paper strip to the tassel and the other to the plate as shown.

Sue Fleischmann; Mary, Queen of Saints School; West Allis, WI

Under the Sea

To wrap up a unit on ocean life, invite each youngster to make an underwater scene.

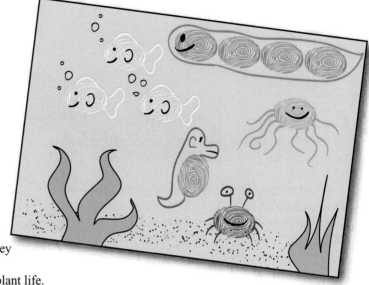

Materials for one scene:
sand
12" x 18" light blue construction paper
construction paper scraps
ink pads in various colors
glue
diluted glue
paintbrush
markers
scissors

Steps:
1. Make several fingerprints on the paper using different colors of ink.
2. Use the markers to add details to the fingerprints so they look like sea creatures.
3. Cut paper scraps so they resemble seaweed and other plant life. Glue them to the paper.
4. Lightly brush diluted glue on the bottom of the paper. Sprinkle sand on the glue and shake off the excess.

Kelsea Wright, Seal Elementary, Douglass, KS

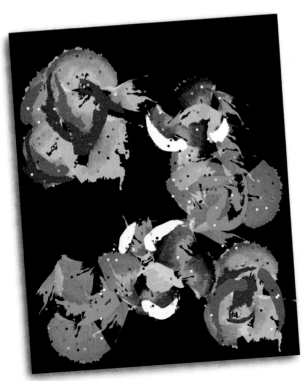

Festive Fireworks
The prints in this project are made by reusing gift bows.

Materials for one project:
9" x 12" black construction paper
gift bows in a variety of shapes and sizes
shallow containers of red, white, and blue paint
silver glitter

Steps:
1. Dip a gift bow in paint. Press the bow onto the paper.
2. Repeat with different bows and colors.
3. While the paint is still wet, sprinkle glitter on the resulting fireworks.
4. After the paint dries, gently shake off the excess glitter.

Sue Fleischmann; Mary, Queen of Saints School; West Allis, WI

TEC42042

TEC42042

Message Cards
Use with "Happy Mother's Day!" on page 14.

I love you from my head to my toes!

I love you from my head to my toes!

©The Mailbox® • TEC42042 • April/May 2009

©The Mailbox® • TEC42042 • April/May 2009

Cap Patterns
Use with "Graduation Buddy" on page 15.

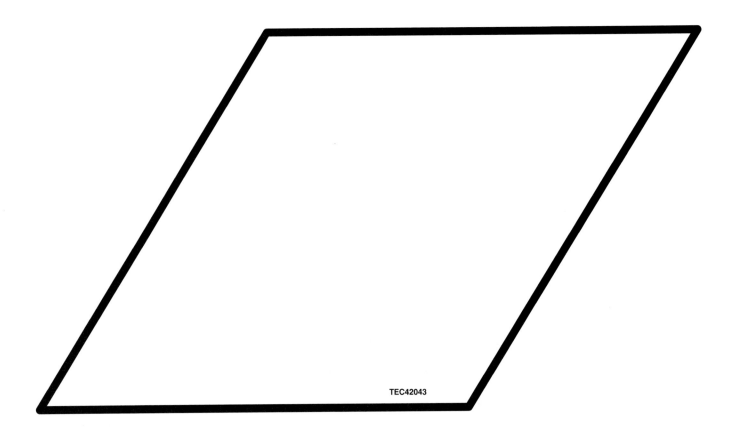

TEC42043

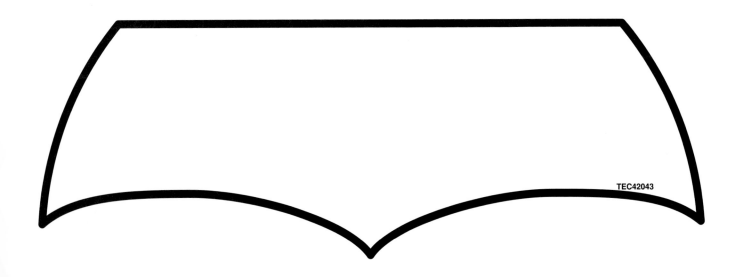

TEC42043

THE BOOK CORNER

Mouse Count
by Ellen Stoll Walsh

An overhead projector makes these follow-up ideas a hit among young students! Gather ten dried kidney beans (mice), a clear plastic cup (jar), and a rubber snake. Turn on an overhead projector and then choose from the options below.

Retelling: Have students use the cup, beans, and snake to act out the story on the projector.

Counting backward: Place the snake near the projector. Put the mice in the cup and then spill them out onto the projector. Have students count backward from ten as you set aside each mouse, in turn.

Addition combinations: Put the snake near the projector. Then place the cup on the projector and set out a number of mice equal to a chosen sum. Guide students to model corresponding addition combinations by putting some mice in the cup and the rest of the mice beside it. List the combinations on the board.

Sheila Criqui-Kelley
Lebo Elementary
Lebo, KS

I remember when Grandma let me help in the garden.

Song and Dance Man
Written by Karen Ackerman
Illustrated by Stephen Gammell

This selection is a perfect choice near National Grandparents Day (the first Sunday after Labor Day). After you read the book aloud, ask students to imagine they each have a trunk like Grandpa does. Invite them to tell what mementos they would put inside. Next, give each youngster a copy of the trunk patterns from page 29. Instruct him to write his name on the line. Have him color the lid and the bottom part of the trunk and then cut out the patterns. Staple the lid to the trunk as shown. Then ask the youngster to open the trunk and illustrate items that remind him of a special time. Encourage him to write a caption or dictate a caption for you to write.
Making connections

The Book Corner

Go Away, Big Green Monster!
By Ed Emberley

Here's a monstrously fun approach to describing words! Read the book to students. Then instruct each child to use a green circle and provided arts-and-crafts supplies to make a monster head on a black sheet of paper. After each child finishes her artwork, revisit the book and draw students' attention to the describing words. Then invite each child to show her monster to the group and use describing words to tell about it. **For more advanced students,** have each youngster write a brief description of her monster. *Describing words*

Jill Tittsworth, Chief Joseph Elementary, Meridian, ID

My monster has big orange eyes. It has blue hair. It looks funny.
Natasha

Bat Jamboree
Written by Kathi Appelt
Illustrated by Melissa Sweet

To prepare this estimating activity, make a number of bat cutouts appropriate for your students' math skills. (For easy preparation, trace a pattern like the one shown on folded black paper.) After you read the book to students, draw on the board a triangle just large enough to hold the cutouts. Tell students that you will make a bat pyramid. Then loosely tape one cutout to the bottom left corner of the triangle. Encourage students to think about the size of the cutout as they estimate how many bats will fit in the triangle. After you record students' estimates, loosely tape the bats to the board to fill the triangle. Then have students compare the actual number of bats with the estimates. *Estimating quantities*

Angie Kutzer, Garrett Elementary, Mebane, NC

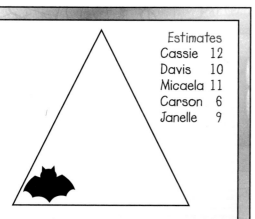

Estimates
Cassie 12
Davis 10
Micaela 11
Carson 6
Janelle 9

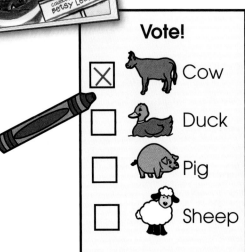

Vote!

☒ Cow

☐ Duck

☐ Pig

☐ Sheep

Duck for President

Written by Doreen Cronin
Illustrated by Betsy Lewin

After you share the book with students, suggest that the class have an election for a new boss of the barnyard. Have students recall the different types of animals in the story; then list the animals on the board to identify the election candidates. Over a few days, encourage each youngster to make a poster for his favorite candidate and ask each of several students to tell the group why he thinks his chosen candidate is the best. On a designated day, have each youngster vote for his favorite candidate by secret ballot. Count the votes with students and record the results on the board. (If there is a tie, determine how to resolve it with student input.) Declare the top vote-getter the boss of the barnyard! ***Participating in a mock election***

Thanksgiving at the Tappletons'

Written by Eileen Spinelli
Illustrated by Megan Lloyd

The Tappletons don't serve up turkey with all the trimmings. Instead, they serve up a reminder of what Thanksgiving is about! After your students are familiar with the story, give each youngster a paper plate. Have her illustrate it to show one or more things for which she is thankful. Invite her to add labels or dictate labels for you to write. Then instruct her to attach the plate, a napkin, and a plastic fork to a sheet of paper and label the paper with her name. Display students' resulting place settings with the title "We Give Thanks!" ***Making connections***

Courtney

my mom and my dog

The Book Corner

The First Day of Winter
By Denise Fleming

Since this delightful story has patterned text, it's perfect for young students to act out. After a first reading, cover two or three plastic toy hoops with white paper. Then attach them to a stack of boxes to make a self-standing snowpal. To identify other needed props, revisit the book with students and make a list of the items the child gives the snowman friend. Arrange for students to gather similar items or make corresponding cutouts. After you gather all the props, encourage students to join in as you read each line, pausing at the appropriate points in the story for youngsters to put the designated items on the snowpal. *Acting out story events*

Jennifer Kay
Van Hise Elementary
Madison, WI

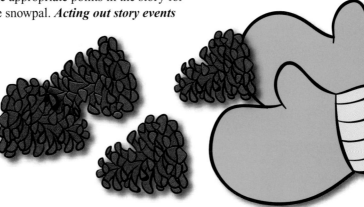

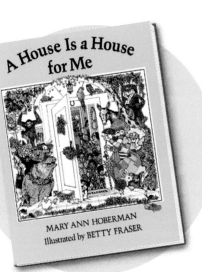

A House Is a House for Me
Written by Mary Ann Hoberman
Illustrated by Betty Fraser

Reinforce both literacy and math with this two-part activity! Read and discuss the book with students. Then give each child a copy of the sentence card from page 30. Help her complete the sentence to tell about a person, an animal, or a thing and a corresponding home. Remind her to punctuate the sentence. Then ask her to glue the sentence card to a sheet of paper and illustrate her work.

Later, display a copy of each category card from page 30 on a folded index card as shown. Place near each card a container with a different color of Unifix cubes. Next, have each student take a cube from the container whose category corresponds with her sentence. Then instruct students to group themselves by cube color. Ask each group to build a tower with its cubes and place it in front of the appropriate card. Then guide youngsters to compare the heights of the towers. ***Completing a sentence, comparing heights***

Melissa Rent, Stonegate Elementary, Zionsville, IN

The Book Corner

Substitute Groundhog

Written by Pat Miller
Illustrated by Kathi Ember

Before reading the story, ask students to share what they know about groundhogs and Groundhog Day. Then explain that in the book, the groundhog needs to find someone to do his job on Groundhog Day. Next, enlist students' help in making a poster to advertise the groundhog's job. To make a poster, glue an enlarged copy of the groundhog pattern (page 175) to a sheet of poster board. Title the poster as shown. Then write a student-generated list of qualities that one must have to work as a groundhog on Groundhog Day. *Activating prior knowledge*

Groundhog Wanted

You need to know what a shadow is.
You need to know when Groundhog Day is.

Franklin's Valentines

Written by Paulette Bourgeois
Illustrated by Brenda Clark

In this class activity, valentine cards fall out of a backpack, just like in the story. Program heart cutouts (valentine cards) with different story elements. Place the cards in an empty backpack. Then role-play the event in which the valentines fall out of Franklin's backpack, allowing the story element cards to fall onto the floor. Next, invite a child to pick up a card and help him read it. Lead students in discussing the named story element. Continue with each remaining card. *Story elements*

Alphabet Adventure
Written by Audrey Wood
Illustrated by Bruce Wood

With this prereading activity, students search to find out which letter is the focus of the story. Use a white crayon to write each lowercase letter on a separate piece of white sentence strip, omitting *i*. Invite each child to use a marker to color a card or two to reveal the letter. Once all the letters are visible, enlist students' help in putting the letters in order. Then ask youngsters to announce the missing letter. After the class determines that *i* is missing, tell them that in the story you are about to read, something happens to the letter *i*. Have students make predictions about what could happen and then read the story aloud. ***Making predictions***

Suzanne Bergstedt
Pumpkin Center Primary
Lincolnton, NC

It Looked Like Spilt Milk
By Charles G. Shaw

Students become authors and artists with this idea to follow up the story. To make an illustration, a student folds a sheet of blue construction paper in half and then unfolds it. Next, she dips a length of thick string into white paint. She arranges the string in a design on one side of her paper. Then she folds the paper over and presses down on top of the string. After unfolding the paper, she removes and discards the string. Finally, she dictates to complete the sentences shown. Bind the completed papers together to make a class book. ***Art, writing***

Kathy Wolford
Mansfield, OH

It looked like a guitar. But it wasn't a guitar. It was a cloud.

It looked like a _____. But it wasn't a _____. It was a _____.

The Book Corner

Fix-It Duck
by Jez Alborough

Fix-It Duck is terrible at fixing things no matter what tool he uses. So no doubt he'll have a difficult time house painting in these student-created stories! Give each child a construction paper copy of the paintbrush pattern on page 31. Read the story starter aloud and invite volunteers to share what they think Duck might do. Encourage each child to finish the story by writing on his paintbrush what he thinks happens. Then have him cut out his brush and glue on a handle cutout. To create a class book, stack the projects behind a cover, hole-punch the handles, and bind the pages with a ring. ***Creating a story innovation***

Tammy Willey
Pine Street Elementary
Presque Isle, ME

Duck looked at his living room wall.
He did not like the color.
This looks like a job for Fix-It Duck!

Duck got paint. He climbed a ladder. The paint fell and made a mess.

This is a job for Fix-It Duck!

Pete's a Pizza
by William Steig

When Pete is in a bad mood, his father cheers him up by making him into a pizza. Have students make pizzas with classmates in a similar way! Prompt youngsters to describe how Pete's dad made the pizza as you write their words on a supersize recipe card. Next, pair students. Then read aloud the recipe as one student in each pair transforms his partner into a pizza using pretend props. Repeat the process, having youngsters switch roles. ***Recalling story details***

Kelsea Wright
Seal Elementary
Douglass, KS

Pete's a Pizza

1. Knead and stretch the dough.
2. Put on some oil and flour.
3. Put on tomatoes and cheese.
4. Tickle the dough.
5. Bake the dough.

The Grouchy Ladybug
by Eric Carle

After a read-aloud of this classic story, invite youngsters to use this project to share their own grouchy moments. First, have each child make black fingerprints on a red semicircle cutout to make a ladybug's body. Direct her to glue to the ladybug a headshot photo of herself with a grouchy expression. Have her glue construction paper legs and antennae to the body. Then give her a speech bubble cutout and help her write about something that makes her grouchy. Display the ladybugs and speech bubbles with the title "Very Grouchy Ladybugs!" ***Making text-to-self connections***

Amanda Burks
Stephanie Cravens Early Childhood Academy
Houston, TX

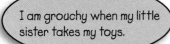

I am grouchy when my little sister takes my toys.

I Want a Pet
by Lauren Child

The narrator of this story debates the drawbacks of many different pets but finally finds one that doesn't have unfortunate habits. Of course, she isn't sure what that pet might be because it's still in an egg! After a read-aloud of the story, give each child a sheet of construction paper with an egg-shaped flap as shown. Prompt each child to lift the flap and draw the creature he imagines is in the egg. Then, on the front of the egg, have him write a description of the creature. ***Extending a story***

Sheila Criqui-Kelley
Lebo Elementary
Lebo, KS

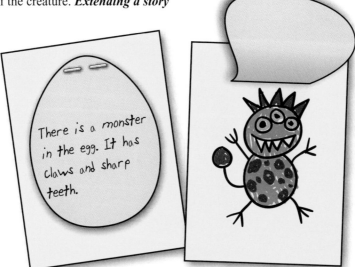

There is a monster in the egg. It has claws and sharp teeth.

The Book Corner

Arthur's Pet Business

By Marc Brown

When Arthur tells his parents he wants a puppy, he proves he is responsible by taking on a pet-sitting business. Have youngsters determine which of Arthur's pet clients is the class favorite with this simple graph. In advance, color and cut out a copy of the picture cards on page 32. Then attach them to a wall graph as shown. After a read-aloud of the story, have students discuss which pet they liked best. Then direct each child to write his name on a sticky note and attach it to the graph. When all the notes are in place, lead students in discussing the results.

Amy Rodriguez, Public School 212, Brooklyn, NY

Favorite Pets

			Charlie	
			Desmond	
			Kara	Jack
	Kate		Bill	Sayid
Courtney	Claire		Jin	Alicia
Debra	Hugo	Aaron	Ben	Stan
dog	canary	ant farm	frogs	boa constrictor

A House for Hermit Crab

By Eric Carle

This classic story about a hermit crab decorating his new shell is segmented into months of the year. Read the story aloud, highlighting the different months. Then tell students they can make a class book describing what they have done over the past few months as well! Present a simple book, as shown, with pages labeled with different months in the school year. Have youngsters help you write appropriate events and accomplishments on each page. Consider attaching cutouts and student drawings to the pages. Then place the book in your independent reading center. Read the book to your new kindergartners next fall to prepare them for the upcoming school year!

Teresa Phillips, Belle Terre Elementary, Palm Coast, FL

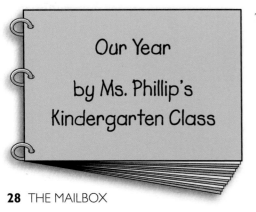

Our Year

by Ms. Phillip's Kindergarten Class

December
We learned the sight words of and to.
We had a holiday party.
The sixth graders helped us make cookies.
We got a new fish in our aquarium.

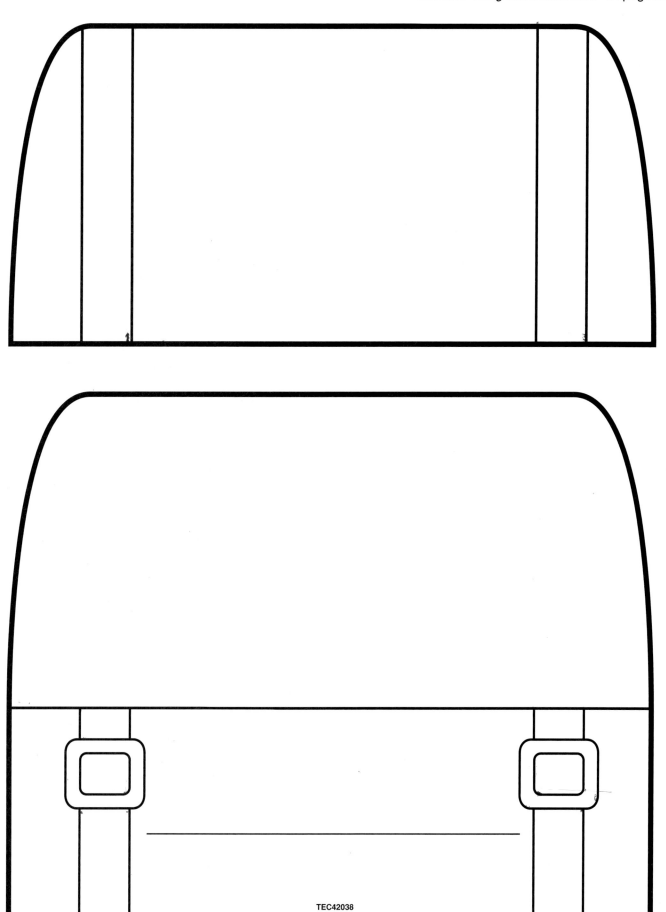

TEC42038

A _____

is a house

for _____

Houses for People

Houses for Animals

Houses for Things

Duck looked at his living room wall.
He did not like the color.
This looks like a job for Fix-It Duck!

TEC42042

Picture Cards

Use with *"Arthur's Pet Business"* on page 28.

dog

TEC42043

canary

TEC42043

ant farm

TEC42043

frogs

TEC42043

boa constrictor

TEC42043

BUILDING MATH SKILLS

Building Math Skills

Shapely Designs

Patterning

For this assessment idea, make a supply of small cutouts of different colors and shapes. (Use scrapbook punches for quick and easy preparation.) Give each student a copy of page 40. Instruct him to arrange chosen cutouts on the paper to make a shape pattern and a color pattern. After you check his work, have him glue the cutouts in place and invite him to color the illustrations. **For more advanced students,** have students draw the patterns rather than make them with cutouts.

Jessica Dauzat
Lafargue Elementary
Effie, LA

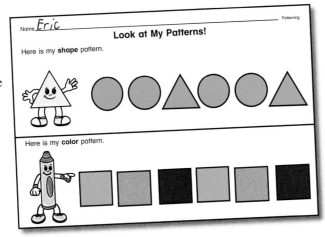

Name Eric
Patterning
Look at My Patterns!
Here is my **shape** pattern.

Here is my **color** pattern.

Hidden by Hives

Beginning subtraction

Try this honey of an idea for modeling subtraction stories! For each child, fold a half sheet of paper (5½" x 8½") in half lengthwise. Cut the top layer of the paper to make five flaps. To begin, ask each child to illustrate a hive on each flap. Next, instruct her to lift each flap, in turn, and make a yellow thumbprint below it. After the thumbprints dry, have her illustrate them to look like bees. Then ask her to unfold all the flaps and model relevant subtraction stories.

Donna Pollhammer
Westminster, MD

There were five bees.
Two bees went in hives.
Three bees are left.

Growing Day by Day

Counting

Here's an adorable way to keep track of how many days of school have passed. Display on a classroom wall a large felt circle that you have decorated to look like a caterpillar's head. On the first day of school, help a youngster label a felt square "1" and then post it beside the caterpillar's head to begin creating a body. On the next school day, help a student add to the caterpillar's body a felt square labeled "2." Invite students to make the caterpillar grow in the same manner each school day. Since the felt will stay bright, the display is sure to be a colorful teaching tool you can use all year for counting by ones, counting backward, and skip-counting!

Deborah Provencher
West Brookfield Elementary
West Brookfield, MA

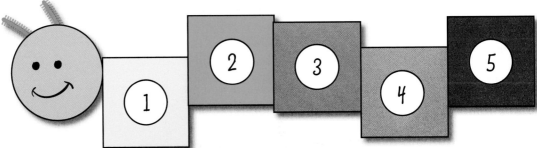

Building Math Skills

Orderly Passengers

Ordinal numbers

For this imaginary train ride, make a train engine cutout and several boxcar cutouts. Write on separate blank cards one ordinal number per cutout, beginning with "1st" and continuing in sequence to match the number of cutouts. Ask a matching number of students (passengers) to sit side by side with the backs of their chairs facing the class. Tape the engine to the back of the first chair and a boxcar to each of the other chairs.

Next, read aloud a chosen ordinal number card. Have students chant "Chug! Chug! Chug!" as a youngster who is not on the train attaches the card to the appropriate train cutout. Then pretend to stop the train and have the passenger in the named seat leave the train. Continue as described until the train is empty.

Linda Edwards
Brinson Memorial School
New Bern, NC

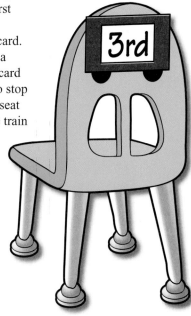

Roll and Sort

Sorting by two attributes

To make dice, cover two cubic boxes with white paper. Then illustrate each side of one box with a different shape and color each side of the other box with a different color. Make a large Venn diagram on the floor with yarn. To play one round, give each child a colorful shape cutout. Invite two students to roll the dice. Then use sticky notes to label the Venn diagram with the shape and color rolled. After each youngster correctly places his cutout on or outside the diagram, discuss the results with students.

Jill Davis
Kendall-Whittier Elementary
Tulsa, OK

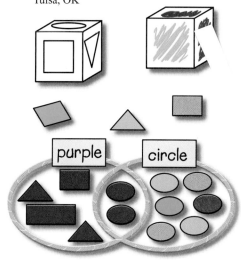

Oops!

Addition

Make a class supply of banana cards (patterns on page 41). Program half the cards with addition combinations and the other half with the corresponding sums so there is one combination or sum per card. To begin, distribute the cards to students at random. Next, have a student with a sum stand and read his card. Then lead the class in saying, "Banana peel, banana peel. Oops, don't fall! Banana peel, banana peel, [sum] in all." Ask each student with a corresponding combination to stand, read it, and then sit with the youngster who has the sum. Help students match the remaining sums and addition combinations in the same manner.

Cathy Wroten
Bear Branch Elementary
Magnolia, TX

Building Math Skills

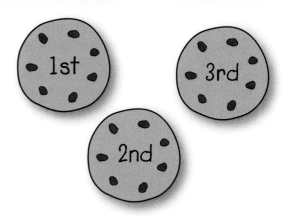

Which Cookie?

Ordinal numbers

For this class activity, label each of ten cookie cutouts with an ordinal number from first to tenth. Store the cookies in a plastic cookie jar or similar container. To play, give each of ten students a cookie from the jar and have the students stand at the front of the room. On your signal, have each child hold his cookie with the number facing the class. Then lead youngsters in the chant shown. Have the named child move to stand in the correct ordinal position. Repeat the chant, inserting each subsequent ordinal number, until each youngster with a cookie is in order.

Teacher: Who took the [first] cookie from the cookie jar?
Students: [Child's name] took the [first] cookie from the cookie jar.

Janet Boyce, Cokato, MN

High Five!

Counting by fives

Use this handy idea to reinforce skip-counting. Give each child ten hand cards (patterns on page 42). Have her write "5" on one card. Then ask her to count the fingers on each hand to help her write increments of five on each remaining card until she reaches 50. After she orders the cards, hole-punch them; then connect them with a binder ring or a length of yarn. Encourage your kindergartners to refer to their cards to help them practice counting by fives.

Yvonne Mausolf, George E. Green Elementary, Bad Axe, MI

A Full Cup

Estimating

For this small-group activity, show students a small cup with ten beans in it. Then give each child an empty cup of the same size and have him predict how many beans it will take to fill the cup. Next, direct him to write his prediction on a copy of the recording sheet from page 42. After he fills his cup with beans, have him count the beans and complete his recording sheet. At another time, repeat the activity with an item of a different size, such as Unifix cubes or bear counters. Lead youngsters to understand that the same cup holds a different number of objects depending on the size of the objects.

Building Math Skills

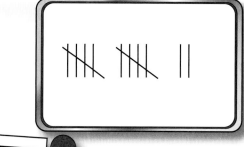

Number of the Day

Number sense

Each day, announce a different number and write it on the board. Provide students with access to manipulatives and individual whiteboards and wipe-off markers. Then invite each student to model the number using a desired method. Encourage youngsters to consider methods such as making tally marks, using ten frames, or writing addition sentences. Invite several students to explain their work to the class.

Brenda Teal
Maxwell Air Force Base Elementary
Maxwell Air Force Base, AL

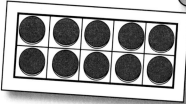

Penny, Nickel, Dime

Coins

Before students recite this change-filled chant, display on the board a model of each coin that is named in the chant. While reciting the chant with youngsters, point to the coin as it is named. As students say the chant, they hold up the number of fingers to correspond to the value of the coin: one finger for *penny,* five fingers for *nickel,* and ten fingers for *dime.*

Penny, nickel, dime,
Penny, nickel, dime.
I see them in a line.
I count them all the time!
Penny, nickel, dime!

Barbara Sudzina, Pulaski Elementary, Pulaski, PA

Crackers for Polly Parrot

Addition

For addition practice that's feathery fun, try this! Have each youngster color and cut out a copy of the mat and cards on page 44. Next, read aloud several addition problems like the one shown. Guide each student to use his mat and cards to model each problem.

Trish Draper, Millarville Community School
Millarville, Alberta, Canada

Polly Parrot eats 2 crackers. Then she eats 4 more crackers. How many crackers does she eat in all?

Building Math Skills

Math Bags

Addition

This activity encourages a home-to-school connection. For each child place in a personalized bag four craft sticks and a card labeled with a number from 2 to 10. Have the child take her bag home and use the materials in the bag as well as small items from home to model an addition sentence like the one shown. Instruct her to pack the objects in her bag and bring the bag to school on a designated day. Encourage each youngster to share her number sentence. Then redistribute the cards to repeat the activity.

Ursula Butler
St. Michael School
North Andover, MA

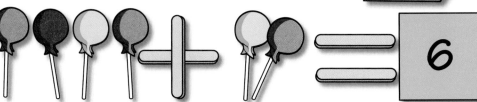

Read the Clock

Time

For this review activity, set the time to the hour on a clock manipulative and then lead the students in singing the song below. At the end of the song, choose a child to name the time on the clock. Then invite him to set the clock to a different time to the hour for another round.

(sung to the tune of "Good Night, Ladies")

> What time is it?
> What time is it?
> What time is it?
> Who can tell me now?

Mary Davis, Keokuk Christian Academy, Keokuk, IA

Colorful Caterpillars

Addition

Prepare for each student an 8½" x 5½" booklet with six pages and a construction paper cover. Give each student a booklet, a copy of page 45, and several sticky dots of two different colors. Instruct the student to cut out the title and problem strips. Then have him glue the title strip to the front cover and glue each problem strip to a separate booklet page. On each page direct him to model the problem by arranging the two colors of sticky dots in a line to make a caterpillar. Then have him count the dots and write the answer. For a finishing touch, invite him to add details to his caterpillars.

Ann Hestand, Watsonville, CA

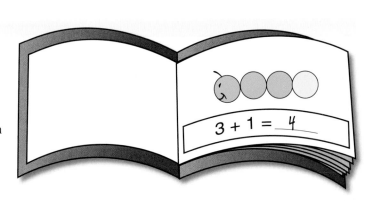

Building Math Skills

Picking Grapes

Counting by tens

Youngsters stretch their math skills with this idea. Have students imagine they are going to pick grapes. Tell them all the grapes they pick are in bunches of ten. As they say each number while counting by tens, have them pantomime stretching up to pick a bunch of grapes.

Carol Kotulan, Faith Baptist School, Kaiserslautern, Germany

Ten, twenty, thirty, forty...

Monkeying Around

Subtraction to ten

Prior to the activity, read aloud the book *Five Little Monkeys Jumping on the Bed* by Eileen Christelow. Then give each student a copy of page 47 and instruct him to cut out the monkey counters and bed workmat. Announce a subtraction word problem involving the monkeys and the bed. Then have youngsters manipulate their monkeys to determine the answer. **For an added challenge,** have students write each subtraction problem on a sheet of paper.

Susan Servin
Oracle Ridge School
Oracle, AZ

Four monkeys are jumping on the bed. Two monkeys fall off. How many monkeys are jumping on the bed now?

Favorite Flavors

Graphing

To prepare for this tasty activity, cut from construction paper a class supply of white circles (ice cream scoops) and two large cones. Label each cone with an ice cream flavor. Have each child write her name on a scoop and color it to match the flavor she would like to eat. Then direct her to place the scoop above the appropriate cone. After all the scoops are on the cones, lead students to gather information from the resulting graph. If desired, conclude the activity by giving students a tasty ice cream treat.

Amy Rodriguez
Public School 212
Brooklyn, NY

See pages 43, 46, and 48 for **skill sheets**.

Name _____

Look at My Patterns!

Here is my **shape** pattern.

Here is my **color** pattern.

Note to the teacher: Use with "Shapely Designs" on page 34.

TEC42039

TEC42039

TEC42039

TEC42039

Hand Cards
Use with "High Five!" on page 36.

TEC42040

TEC42040

TEC42040

TEC42040

Estimating

Name _____

A Full Cup

I think the cup will hold _____ beans.

The cup held _____ beans.

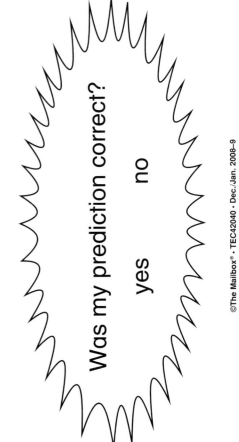

Was my prediction correct?

yes   no

©The Mailbox® • TEC42040 • Dec./Jan. 2008–9

Note to the teacher: Use the recording sheet with "A Full Cup" on page 36.

Marching Band

Write the missing numbers.

| 6 | 7 | ___ | 9 | ___ |

| 15 | ___ | 17 | ___ | ___ | 20 |

| 8 | ___ | ___ | 11 | ___ |

| 10 | 11 | ___ | ___ | 14 |

| 2 | ___ | 4 | ___ | ___ |

Crackers for Polly Parrot

©The Mailbox® • TEC42041 • Feb./Mar. 2009

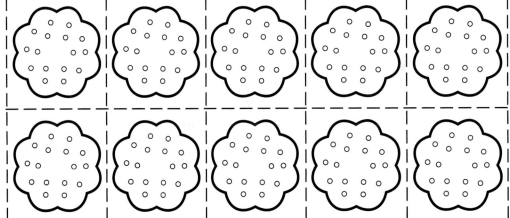

Note to the teacher: Use with "Crackers for Polly Parrot" on page 37.

Caterpillar Addition

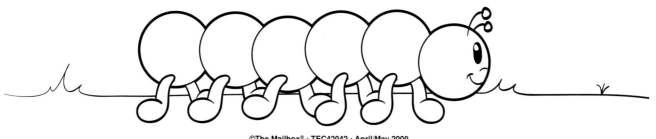

©The Mailbox® • TEC42042 • April/May 2009

1 + 2 = _____
TEC42042

2 + 3 = _____
TEC42042

3 + 1 = _____
TEC42042

2 + 6 = _____
TEC42042

3 + 3 = _____
TEC42042

5 + 2 = _____
TEC42042

Flowers for Sale

Name _____

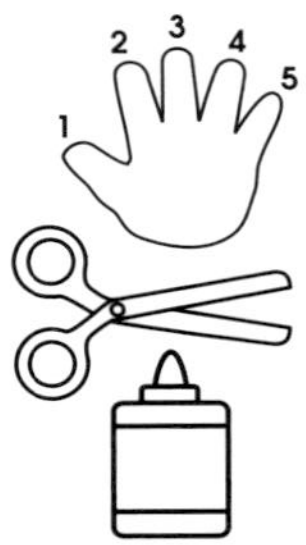

Count.
Cut.
Glue to match.

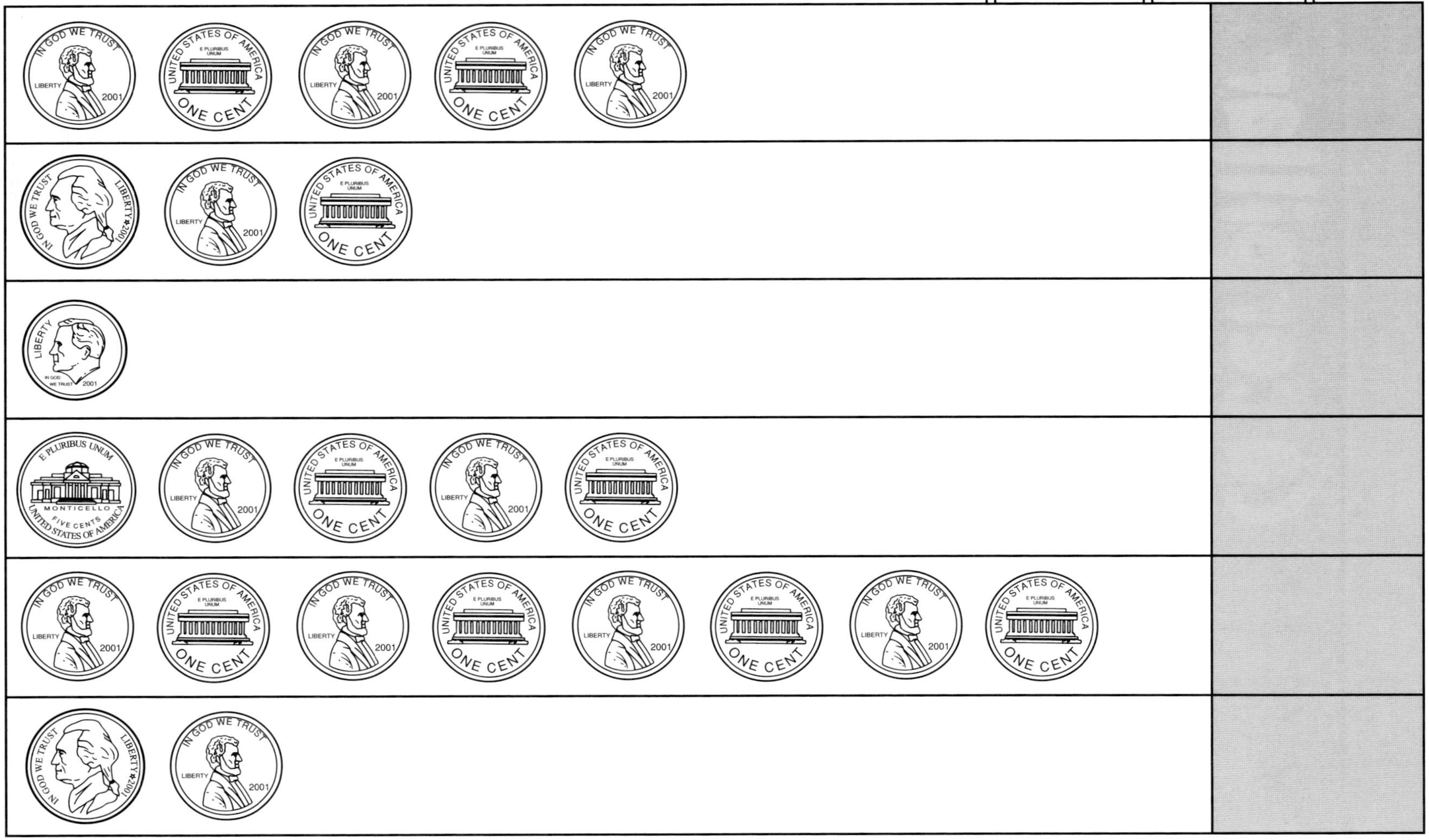

9¢

8¢

6¢

7¢

5¢

10¢

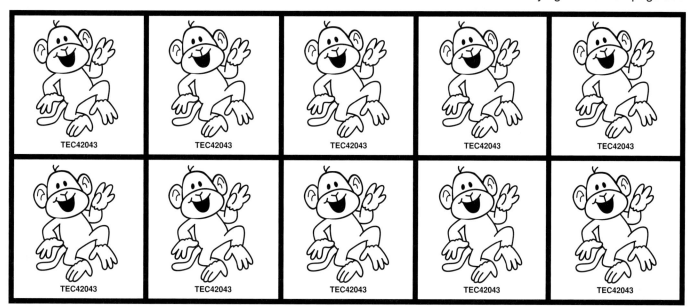

TEC42043 TEC42043 TEC42043 TEC42043 TEC42043

TEC42043 TEC42043 TEC42043 TEC42043 TEC42043

©The Mailbox® • TEC42043 • June/July 2009

A Sundae for Mouse

🖍 Color the cubes.

Reproducible partner game: Use with the directions on page 51.

THE MAILBOX **49**

Jake's Cakes

Equal Parts	Unequal Parts

©The Mailbox® • TEC42040 • Dec./Jan. 2008–9

Reproducible partner game: Use with the directions on page 51.

Hide and Seek!

What You Need
gameboard
2 game markers
die
2 sheets of paper

How to play:

1. Play with a partner. Put your game markers on START.
2. Roll the die, in turn, and move your marker.
3. Read the number you land on. Write it on your paper.
4. The first player to reach FINISH wins.

©The Mailbox® • TEC42040 • Dec./Jan. 2008–9

Jake's Cakes

Skill: Identifying equal and unequal parts

What You Need
2 gameboards
2 game markers
die
2 crayons

How to play:

1. Play with a partner. Put your game markers on the bowl.
2. Roll a die, in turn, and move your marker to a cake.
3. Tell whether the cake has equal or unequal parts. Then color a matching box.
4. The first player to color all the boxes in one column wins. (You may need to go around the board more than once.)

©The Mailbox® • TEC42040 • Dec./Jan. 2008–9

Note to the teacher: Use "Hide and Seek!" with page 49 and "Jake's Cakes" with page 50.

Follow the Fish!

Start counting with me!

1st

2nd

3rd

4th

5th

6th

7th

8th

9th

10th

Reproducible partner game: Use with the directions on page 54.

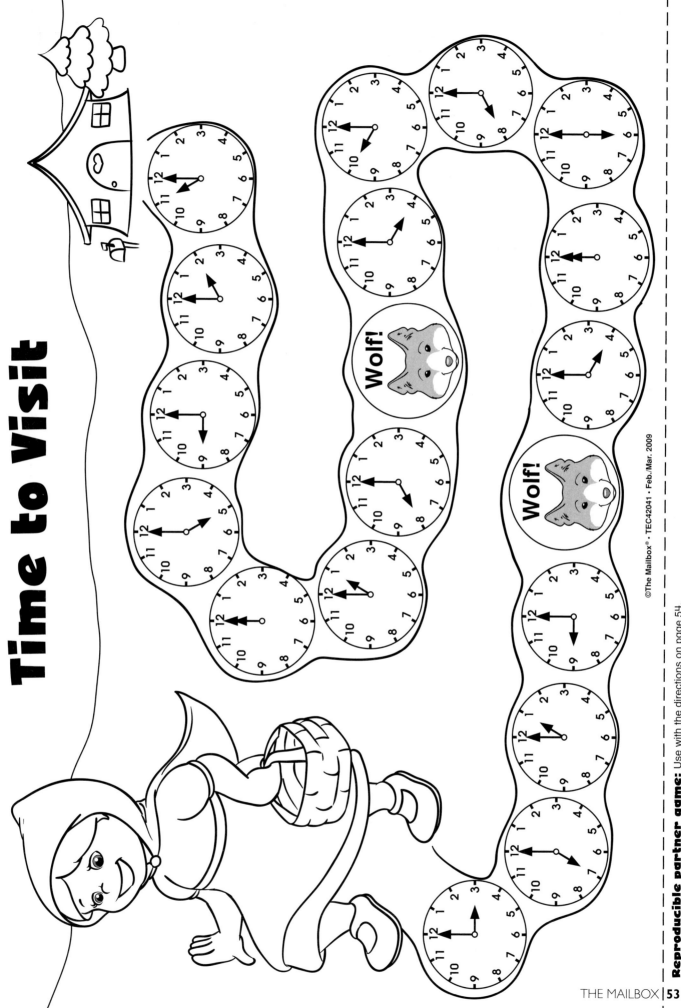

Time to Visit

Wolf!

Wolf!

Reproducible partner game: Use with the directions on page 54.

Follow the Fish!

What You Need
2 gameboards
paper clip
pencil
crayons

How to play:
1. Play with a partner.
2. Spin, in turn.
   If the spinner lands on , name a fish
   by its ordinal number and color it.
   If the spinner lands on ☹, your turn
   is over.
3. The first player to color all his fish wins.

©The Mailbox® • TEC42041 • Feb./Mar. 2009

Time to Visit

Skill: Time to the hour

What You Need
gameboard
2 game markers
labeled counter

How to play:
1. Play with a partner. Put the game
   markers on Little Red Riding Hood.
2. Toss the counter, in turn, and move
   your marker.
3. If you land on a clock, read the time.
   If you land on 🐺, go ahead 1 space.
   Read the time.
4. The first player to reach the house wins.

©The Mailbox® • TEC42041 • Feb./Mar. 2009

Gum Chums!

Take away
1

Take
away
4

Take
away
2

Take away
3

Shep's Shapes

cylinder

sphere

cone

cube

Reproducible partner game: Use with the directions on page 57.

Gum Chums!

How to play:

1. Play with a partner.
2. Spin, in turn. Cross out the matching number of gumballs in the first row. Say the take-away sentence.
3. Repeat Step 2 for each row.
4. Color the gumballs that are left. The player with more colored gumballs wins.

What You Need
2 gameboards
2 crayons
paper clip
pencil

©The Mailbox® • TEC42042 • April/May 2009

Shep's Shapes

Skill: Solid figures

How to play:

1. Play with a partner.
2. Spin, in turn, and name the shape.
3. Color a matching shape. If there is no matching shape to color, your turn is over.
4. The first player to color all his shapes wins.

What You Need
2 gameboards
2 crayons
paper clip
pencil

©The Mailbox® • TEC42042 • April/May 2009

Name _____

Hop to It!

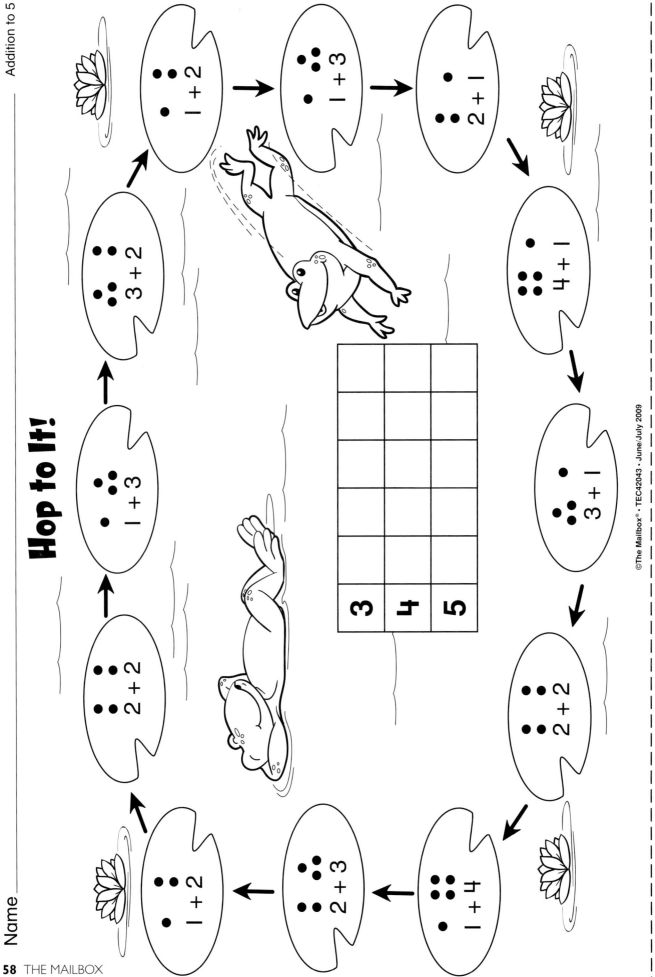

1 + 2

1 + 3

2 + 1

4 + 1

3 + 2

1 + 3

2 + 2

3 + 1

2 + 2

1 + 2

2 + 3

1 + 4

| 3 |
| 4 |
| 5 |

Reproducible partner game: Use with the directions on page 60.

Name

Chow Time!

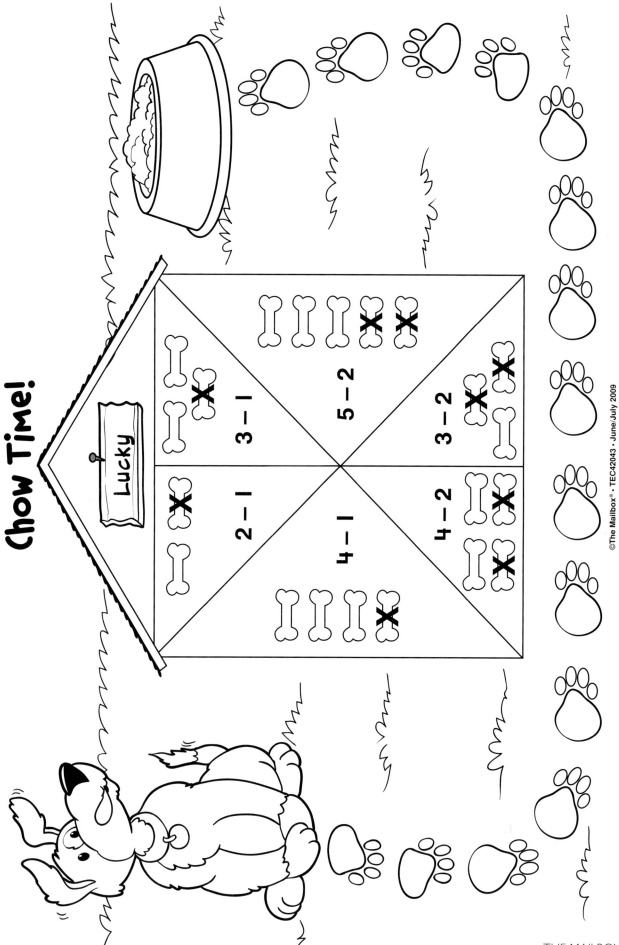

Lucky

3 – 1

5 – 2

3 – 2

2 – 1

4 – 1

4 – 2

©The Mailbox® • TEC42043 • June/July 2009

Reproducible partner game: Use with the directions on page 60.

Hop to It!

Skill: Addition to 5

How to play:

1. Play with a partner. Put your markers on a lily pad.
2. When it is your turn, roll the die and move your marker.
3. Read the problem. Say the sum. Color a matching box.
4. The first player to color all the boxes in one row wins.

What You Need

2 gameboards
2 game markers
die
2 crayons

©The Mailbox® • TEC42043 • June/July 2009

Chow Time!

Skill: Subtraction to 5

How to play:

1. Play with a partner.
2. When it is your turn, spin. Say the problem.
3. Say the answer. Color that many .
4. The first player to color all his wins.

What You Need

2 gameboards
paper clip
pencil
2 crayons

©The Mailbox® • TEC42043 • June/July 2009

Note to the teacher: Use with the gameboards on pages 58 and 59.

CLASSROOM DISPLAYS

CLASSROOM DISPLAYS

Count on open house guests to go wild over this idea! Help each child make a construction paper animal head and then cut out an oval for the face. Attach a photo of the child to the animal head so the child's face shows through the opening. Showcase the animals with the title shown. During open house, challenge parents to identify their children's photos.

Candy McCormick, Mohawk Elementary, Bessemer, PA

For this year-round display, write each youngster's name and birthdate on a banana cutout. Then arrange the bananas in a bunch hanging from a tree. (See the banana and stem patterns on page 70.) Add a title, a monkey head, and two monkey hands. At the beginning of each month, highlight the upcoming birthdays by attaching the corresponding bananas to the monkey's hands.

Meagan Waters
The Discovery School
Gambrills, MD

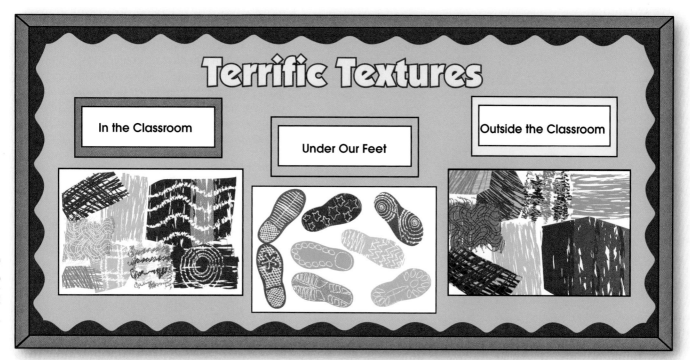

Here's a fun idea to add to your five senses unit. Have students use crayons to do rubbings of various items in the classroom and outside of the classroom. Make a collage of each set of rubbings. Also ask each youngster to do a rubbing of the sole of his shoe, cut out the rubbing, and then mount it on a poster. Display the rubbings as desired.

Diane Awakuni, Koko Head School, Honolulu, HI

To make a horse, tack crumpled tissue paper to a board as shown. Then add strips of tissue paper for the tail, mane, and hooves. Dress a cardboard head-and-torso cutout to make a rider. Position the rider on the horse and add cardboard arms. To complete the display, frame students' photos or names with horseshoe cutouts (pattern on page 70) and post a title.

Donna A. Davidson, B. P. S. Kindergarten, Ringgold, GA

CLASSROOM DISPLAYS

The Book Patch

After a student listens to a read-aloud or reads a story, have him complete an orange copy of the book report form from page 71 and color the pumpkin stem. Display youngsters' completed forms with leaf cutouts and crepe paper streamers (vines) as desired. No doubt youngsters will be eager to make the patch of pumpkins grow throughout the fall!

Darlene Martin
South Elementary
Hingham, MA

Name _David_

Title: _Barnyard Banter_

Author: _Denise Fleming_

The best part of the story was when _the goose chased the dragonfly._

Pumpkin-Seed Book Rating

okay   good   great

Look What Followed Us to School!

Mary had a little lamb, and _Austin_ had a _perfect pig._

Mary had a little lamb, and _Roger_ had a _happy hippo._

Mary had a little lamb, and _Marco_ had a _terrific tiger._

Mary had a little lamb, and _Sidney_ had a _big bear._

Whether you use this idea as a nursery rhyme follow-up or as part of a describing word unit, it's sure to please! Have each student make an animal using a disposable animal plate and chosen arts-and-crafts supplies. Then help her complete a caption, like the ones shown, with her name and an alliterative animal phrase. Display students' one-of-a-kind critters with the captions and a title.

Cheri Adair, Merkel Elementary, Merkel, TX

Warm Up With a Good Book

This board is a great follow-up to a wintry class read-aloud. Select a story with a clear beginning, middle, and end. After sharing the story, have each child write or draw on each of three separate mitten cutouts to tell a different part of the story. Instruct him to place his mittens behind a construction paper cover and write his name on the cover. Hole-punch the pages and secure them with yarn. Then hang the booklets on a fireplace scene similar to the one shown.

Catherine Cliver, Bernice Young Elementary, Burlington, NJ

❄ Estimation Station ❄

Provide estimation practice at this cool, interactive display. To make a snowpal, each child glues paper circles together, draws facial details, and glues on cotton balls. Next, he counts how many cotton balls he used and writes the number inside a folded hat shape. After checking for accuracy, post the snowpals with their corresponding hats on an easy-to-reach display. A student estimates the number of cotton balls on a snowpal and lifts the hat to see how close he was to the actual number.

Stefanie Burns, NMSS, Pleasantville, NJ

Your youngsters will be eager to lend a hand in creating this display, which honors Dr. Martin Luther King Jr. Glue a copy of the Dr. King pattern on page 72 to the center of a large paper heart and add the title shown. Following a discussion about Dr. King's dream of peace, have each youngster cut out a pair of skin-toned hand patterns and glue them to the edge of the heart. Then post the heart as a friendly reminder of Dr. King's dream.

Debbie Hill, Stone Elementary, Crossville, TN

Paper shapes make it easy to create this wintry display! Have each child glue a trimmed photo of herself to the center of a paper oval. Instruct her to glue the oval and precut paper rectangles to resemble a snowsuit as shown. After she glues on cotton ball "fur," help her cut out and glue on mittens and boots. Then display students' self-likenesses on a snowy backdrop.

Nikki Buwalda, Randolph Elementary, Randolph, WI

CLASSROOM DISPLAYS

Students practice estimation using this display prepared in honor of Dr. Seuss's birthday (March 2). Invite youngsters to cut several handprints from red and white construction paper. Glue the handprints to a sheet of bulletin board paper to make a striped hat as shown. Using their own hands as guides, have each child estimate how many handprints it took to make the hat. After comparing the estimates and the actual total, point out how the different sizes of the handprints influenced the total.

Abby Clark, Sandoval Grade School, Sandoval, IL

Have each youngster color and cut out a copy of either the lion pattern on page 73 or the lamb pattern on page 74. Then cut out the face of each critter where indicated and attach a photo of the child. Help each student write a sentence about March on a blank card. Then display each child's critter with his sentence.

Susan Doss Quarles, New London Academy, Forest, VA

CLASSROOM DISPLAYS

It's Raining Word Families

-an

-ap

can

man

tan

pan

fan

tap

lap

cap

map

nap

Provide extra practice reading word family words with this rainy-day scene. Post the title, two cloud shapes, and a large umbrella cutout as shown. Then label each cloud with a different rime. Brainstorm with youngsters words in each word family and write each response on an individual raindrop cutout. Then display the raindrops below the matching clouds.

Michelle House, McKitrick Elementary, Lutz, FL

Picture-Perfect Spring

Kindergarten happenings are on display with these blooms! Provide class-related photographs of your students. Have each child glue large paper circles, hearts, or ovals (petals) to the back of a small paper plate to form a flower bloom. Then help him glue a photo to the plate and add a stem and leaves. Arrange the flowers and a title on a wall to create a memorable springtime scene.

Tawn Snyder, Northwest Elementary, Dodge City, KS

CLASSROOM DISPLAYS

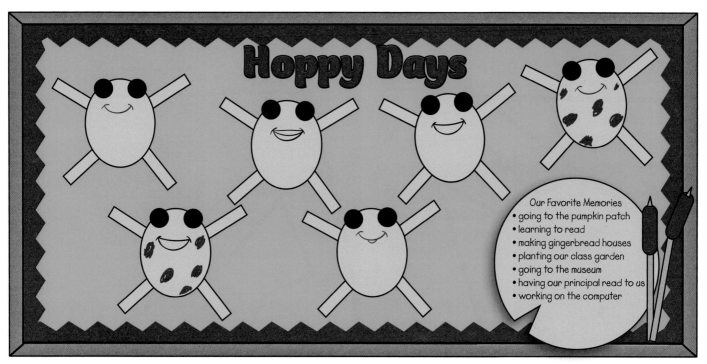

Students share their "hoppy" memories from the school year on this end-of-the-year display. Have each child glue four green paper rectangles (legs) and two black paper circles (eyes) to a green oval (body). After she draws a mouth and other desired details, post the frog on a board titled as shown. Then record students' favorite memories on a large paper lily pad and post the lily pad with a few cattails for decoration.

Diane Bonica, Deer Creek Elementary, Tigard, OR

Kindergartners' heights are on display with these blooms! Have each child draw facial details similar to his own on a paper circle. Then direct him to glue paper ovals around the face so they resemble petals. Mount each flower to a wall to show the child's height. Then have him add green paper strips to make a stem. If desired, add leaves and grass. Lead youngsters in using the resulting display to measure and compare their heights.

Angela Allard, Southern Pines, NC

Stem and Banana Patterns
Use with "Birthday Bunch" on page 62.

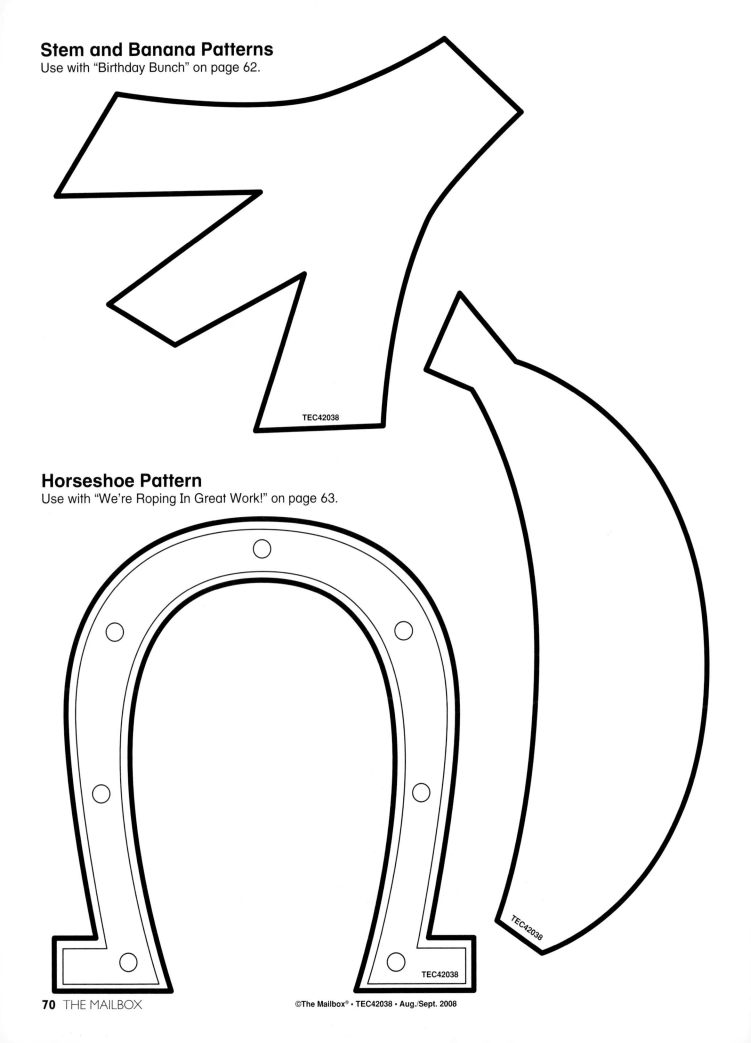

TEC42038

Horseshoe Pattern
Use with "We're Roping In Great Work!" on page 63.

TEC42038

TEC42038

Book Report Form

Use with “The Book Patch” on page 64.

Name ____

Title: ____

Author: ____

The best part of the story was when ________________

____

____

Pumpkin-Seed Book Rating

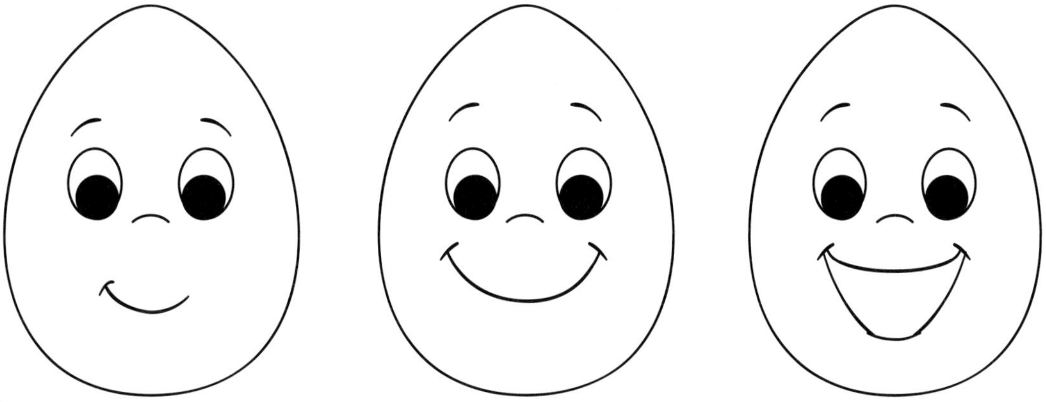

okay **good** **great**

TEC42039

Dr. Martin Luther King Jr. Pattern

Use with "I Have a Dream" on page 66.

TEC42040

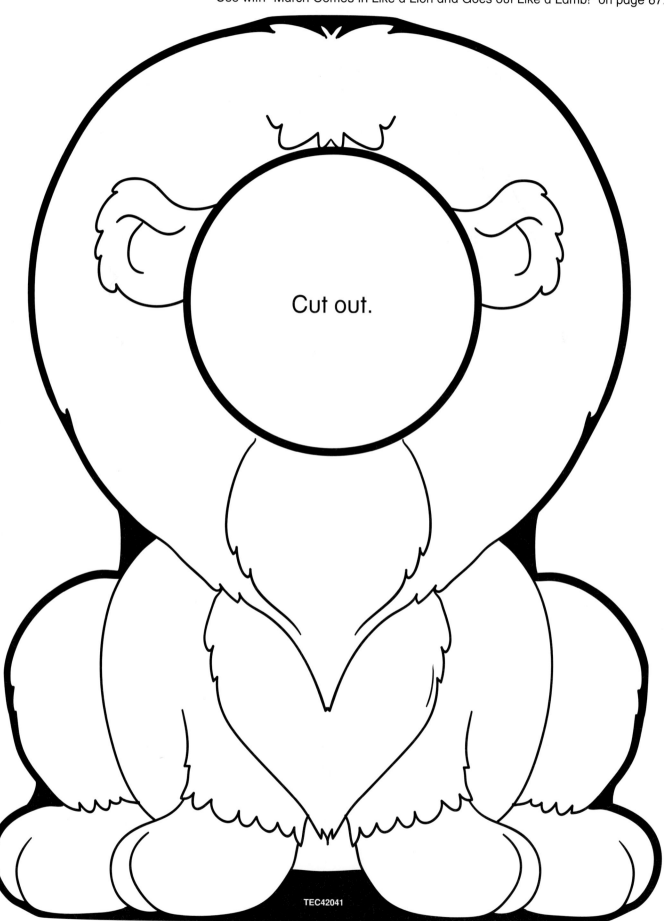

Cut out.

TEC42041

Lamb Pattern

Use with "March Comes in Like a Lion and Goes out Like a Lamb!" on page 67.

Cut out.

TEC42041

LEARNING CENTERS

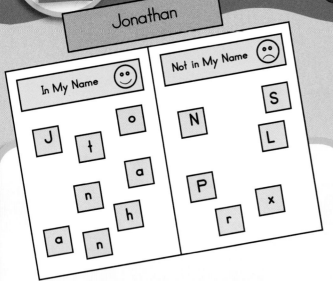

Jonathan

Namely, Sorting
Literacy Center

To prepare this letter-perfect activity, divide and label a sheet of paper as shown. Place the prepared paper, a class supply of name cards, and a supply of letter cards at a center. To complete the activity, a youngster sets his name card above the labeled paper. Then he sorts the letter cards into the appropriate columns, attending to the uppercase and lowercase forms of the letters. *Letter recognition*

Jayne E. Jaskolski
21st Street School
Milwaukee, WI

Packaged for Reading
Literacy Center

Show youngsters that they are already readers with this brand-name book! Mount several familiar food labels and box fronts on separate sheets of construction paper. Laminate the papers. Then bind them between two covers and title the resulting book as desired. Invite each center visitor to read the book independently or with a partner. **For more advanced students,** write a chosen letter or word on each page before laminating it. Have students use a wipe-off marker to circle the designated letters and words. *Environmental print*

Jean Ricotta, Paumanok Elementary, Dix Hills, NY

Counting Sheep
Math or Literacy Center

What makes this activity a "shear" delight? It's easy to adapt for different skills! Mount several copies of the sheep cards from page 83 on colorful paper and choose an option below.

Modeling numbers: Write a different number on each sheep. A youngster puts the designated number of cotton balls on each card.

Addition: Write an addition problem on each sheep and set out a supply of paper. A student models the problems with cotton balls and writes each corresponding number sentence.

Phonological awareness: Glue a copy of a picture card from page 83 on each sheep. Write on the back of each sheep card the number of syllables in the corresponding word. A student names each word, claps once for each syllable, and then puts the matching number of cotton balls on the sheep. To check her work, she clears each card, in turn, and flips it.

Tiffini Ann Amato, The Center for Discovery, Harris, NY

Learning Centers

Shake It Up!
Literacy or Math Center

Choose an option below and program 12 sticky dots as described. Adhere each dot to a different cup of a sanitized foam egg carton. Then place a pom-pom in the carton and close it. Place the carton at a center stocked with paper. A student shakes the carton and then opens it. After she reads the sticky dot on which the pom-pom landed, she completes the activity as described below.

Letter-sound associations: Write a letter on each sticky dot. A child draws pictures whose names begin with the indicated letter.
Word families: Write a rime on each sticky dot. A child lists words that contain the indicated rime.
Addition: Write a number (sum) on each sticky dot. A child illustrates and writes corresponding addition combinations.

Daina Flores, Sunset Ridge Elementary
Pacifica, CA

Hands-On Reading
Literacy Center

This activity requires nearly no advance preparation! Place some play dough and two or three vinyl placemats near your word wall. Arrange for two or three students to complete the activity at one time. Have each youngster use the play dough to form words on a placemat and then ask the other students at the center to read them. ***Reading and spelling words***

Beth Kickert
T. C. Cherry Elementary
Bowling Green, KY

Ten-Frame Treasure
Math Center

Here's a kid-pleasing approach to counting sets! Purchase an inexpensive treasure chest or decorate a box to make one. Then put in the chest up to 15 of each of the following items: plastic gems, colorful bow-tie pasta, imitation pennies, paper clips, large buttons, and counters. Place the chest, a piece of felt (workmat), and student copies of page 84 at a center. When a student visits the center, he colors the workmat. Then he sorts the treasures and uses the ten frame on his paper to count them. He writes the corresponding numbers where indicated. ***Counting to 15***

Susan Robinson
North Ridge Primary School
Commack, NY

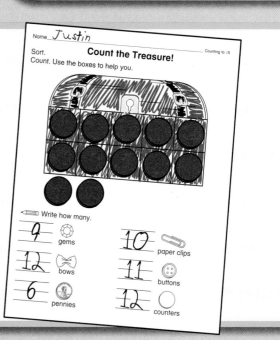

Learning Centers

Bring On the Buttons!
Math Center

Build counting or addition skills with a frosty friend! Make a paper snowman with a face and a top hat. Program several sticky notes for an option described below. Place the sticky notes, the snowman, and a supply of small craft foam or tagboard circles (buttons) at a center. Have students complete the activity as described.

Counting: Write a different number on each sticky note. A student attaches a sticky note to the snowman's hat and then places the matching number of buttons on the snowman.

Concept of addition: Write a different addition problem on each sticky note. A student attaches a sticky note to the snowman's hat and places the corresponding number of buttons on the snowman to solve the problem.

Kristi Miller
Woodward-Granger Elementary
Granger, IA

All in Order
Math Center

To prepare, program a copy of the calendar on page 85 with the name of the current month; then laminate the calendar. Using a dry-erase marker, draw a star on the first day of the month. Then use the marker to fill in a desired number of dates. Place the calendar at a center along with a cut-out copy of the calendar cards from page 86. A student places the cards on the calendar in the correct order. Adjust the difficulty of the center by programming the calendar with more or fewer dates. *Calendar, number order*

Cindee Grijalva, Bonham Elementary, Houston, TX

What's Inside?
Literacy Center

Color a copy of the center mat on page 87 and a copy of the activity cards on page 88. Code the backs of the ending sound cards to make the activity self-checking. Put the cards in a resealable plastic bag. To complete the activity, a student stacks the cards beside her mat. She names the picture on the top card and then places the card in the box below the item with the same ending sound. After she sorts the remaining cards, she flips the cards to check her work. *Ending sounds*

Catherine Broome-Kehm
Melbourne Beach, FL

Learning Centers

Alphabet Soup
Literacy Center

Serve up a perfect portion of practice with letters and sounds! In a large soup pot, place small objects or pictures of items that begin with different letters. Place the pot, a ladle, and an alphabet chart at a center. A student uses the ladle to scoop out one object or picture. Then she names the item, emphasizing its beginning sound, and places it on the corresponding letter on the chart. She continues as time allows or until the pot is empty. *Letter-sound correspondence*

Robbye Spector, P. S. #29 Annex, Jersey City, NJ

Swat It!
Literacy or Math Center

Program several cards and a sheet of poster board for an option described below. Place the poster board, the cards, a clean flyswatter, and paper at a center. Have each student complete the activity as described.

Sight words: Program the cards with different sight words. Then write the matching words on the poster board. For each card, a student reads the word and swats the matching word on the poster board. For more practice, she also writes the word on a sheet of paper.

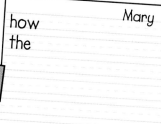

Counting: Program the cards with different amounts of dots. Then write the matching numbers on the poster board. For each card, a student counts the dots and swats the matching number on the poster board. Then she writes the number on a sheet of paper and draws the corresponding number of dots.

Mandy Leach
Locust Grove Early Learning Center
Locust Grove, OK

Same-Size Slices
Math Center

For this fraction center, gather several cookie cutters in shapes that can be divided into two equal parts. Place the cookie cutters, play dough, and nonserrated plastic knives at a center. A youngster uses a cookie cutter to make a shape in the play dough. Then he uses the knife to cut the shape into two equal parts. Next, he compares the two pieces to see if they are equal in size and shape. If he is satisfied, he traces the cookie cutter on a sheet of paper and draws a line to show where he cut the shape. He continues making more shapes as time allows. *Equal parts*

Courtney Pate, Burlington, NC

Learning Centers

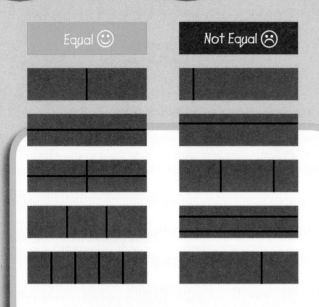

| Equal ☺ | Not Equal ☹ |

Candy Bars to Share?
Math Center

Cut several rectangles (candy bars) from brown construction paper. Use a marker to divide some candy bars into equal parts and the rest into unequal parts. Make two labels like the ones shown. Place the labels and the candy bars at a center. A child uses the labels to sort each candy bar. *Equal and unequal parts*

Soup Scoop
Literacy Center

Give youngsters a heaping helping of number word practice. Number ten disposable bowls from 1 to 10; then turn over the bowls and label the bottom of each bowl with the corresponding number word. Place inside each bowl the letter manipulatives needed to spell the number word and a plastic spoon. A student scoops the letters from a bowl and uses them to spell the number word. Then she turns the bowl over to check her work. She returns the letters and spoon to the bowl and continues with the remaining bowls. *Number words*

Lydia Hess
Chambersburg, PA

Doggy Dig
Literacy and Math Center

For a sight word activity youngsters will really dig, try this! Cut apart a laminated copy of the bone cards on page 89 and bury them in a container filled with sand. Place at a center the container, copies of the recording sheet from page 89, and digging tools. A student digs up a word and reads it. He then makes a tally mark beside the word on his sheet and returns the word to the sand. After a designated amount of time, he counts each group of tallies and writes the number on his sheet. *Sight words, tally marks*

Jody Carlson
Smith Elementary
Berea, OH

Name: Sam — Recording sheet

Word	Tally Marks	Total
and	I	
can		
for		
go		
have		
me		
see	II	
the		
up		

see

Learning Centers

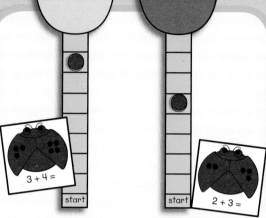

Ladybug Addition
Math Center

For this partner game, prepare two flower gameboards like the ones shown and cut apart a copy of the addition cards on page 90. Place at a center the gameboards, the cards in a face-down stack, and two red counters (ladybugs). Each player puts her ladybug at the bottom of her gameboard. Then each child takes a card from the stack and names the sum. Her partner checks her work by counting the ladybug's spots. The player with the larger sum moves her ladybug one space. Players continue, shuffling the cards as needed, until one ladybug reaches its flower. *Addition to ten*

Lauren Harms, Oakland, CA

Neighborhood of Words
Literacy Center

To prepare this word-building activity, decorate several empty cereal boxes to resemble houses. Label each house with a different rime. For each house, program tagboard squares with different consonants that will form words with the rime. Place each set in its matching house. A child removes the squares from the house and, in turn, places each square in front of the rime and reads the resulting word. **For an added challenge,** he writes each word on a sheet of paper. *Word families*

adapted from an idea
  by Glenda Furtick
Busbee Elementary
Wagener, SC

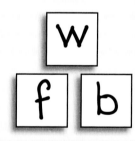

Bee and Flowers
Math Center

Students will be all abuzz about skip-counting with this idea. Label a supply of flower cutouts with numbers used in a skip-counting sequence. Also make a bee pointer like the one shown. Place the pointer and flowers at a center. A student arranges the flowers to show the number sequence. Then she names each number as she "flies" the bee over the flowers. *Skip-counting*

Learning Centers

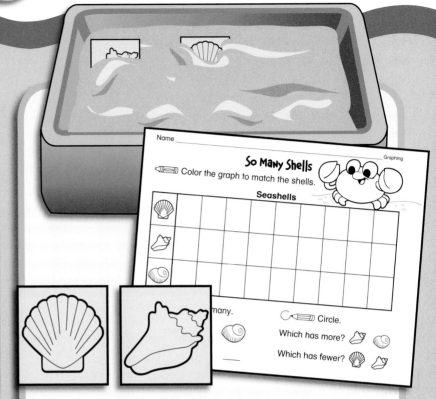

Spelling Box
Literacy Center

Label each index card in a supply with a different CVC word; on the other side of the card, glue or draw a matching picture. Store the cards in an index card file box with the pictures facing forward. Place the box at a center along with a whiteboard and a wipe-off marker. A student takes a card, lays it picture-side up, and then writes the word on the board. He turns the card over to check his answer. Then he repeats the activity with the remaining cards. *Spelling*

Susan Brown, Central Elementary, Palmyra, VA

Digging for Shells
Math Center

Cut apart several copies of the shell cards on page 91 and laminate them for durability. Then bury a different number (less than ten) of each card in a tub of sand. Place the tub at a center along with plastic digging tools and a class supply of the graphing sheet on page 91. A child digs up the shells, sorts them by type, and completes a graphing sheet. Then she buries the cards to prepare the center for the next student. *Graphing*

Angie Kutzer, Garrett Elementary, Mebane, NC

Happy Campers
Literacy Center

For a fun camping-themed center, color a copy of the center mat on page 92 and a copy of the activity cards on page 93. Code the backs of the sequence cards to make the activity self-checking. Put each set in a separate resealable plastic bag. To complete the activity, a student spreads out one set of cards faceup. She arranges the cards in order on the mat and then flips her cards to check her work. She repeats the activity with the remaining card sets. **For more advanced students,** after a youngster checks her work, have her write about the pictures using words such as *first, next,* and *last.* *Sequencing*

Catherine Broome-Kehm, Melbourne Beach, FL

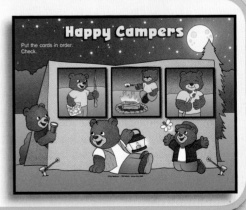

TEC42038

TEC42038

TEC42038

TEC42038

Picture Cards
Use with the phonological awareness option for "Counting Sheep" on page 76.

Count the Treasure!

Sort.
Count. Use the boxes to help you.

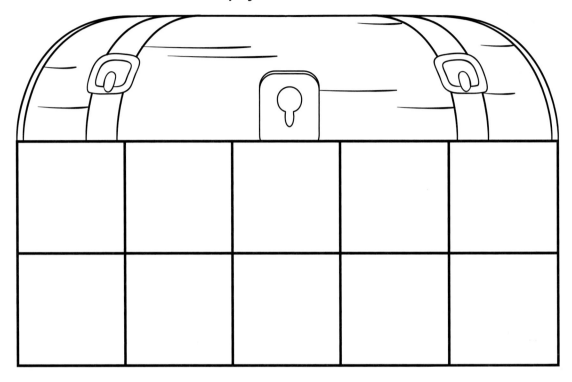

✏ Write how many.

_____ ⬡ gems   _____ 📎 paper clips

_____ bows   _____ buttons

_____ pennies   _____ counters

Note to the teacher: Use with "Ten-Frame Treasure" on page 77.

	Sunday	Monday	Tuesday	Wednesday	Thursday	Friday	Saturday
(month)							

Note to the teacher: Use with "All in Order" on page 78.

Calendar Cards
Use with "All in Order" on page 78.

7	14	21	28	
6	13	20	27	
5	12	19	26	
4	11	18	25	
3	10	17	24	31
2	9	16	23	30
1	8	15	22	29

 ©The Mailbox® • TEC42040 • Dec./Jan. 2008–9

What's Inside?

Sort by ending sounds.
Check.

©The Mailbox® • TEC42040 • Dec./Jan. 2008–9

Activity Cards
Use with "What's Inside?" on page 78.

©The Mailbox® • TEC42040 • Dec./Jan. 2008–9

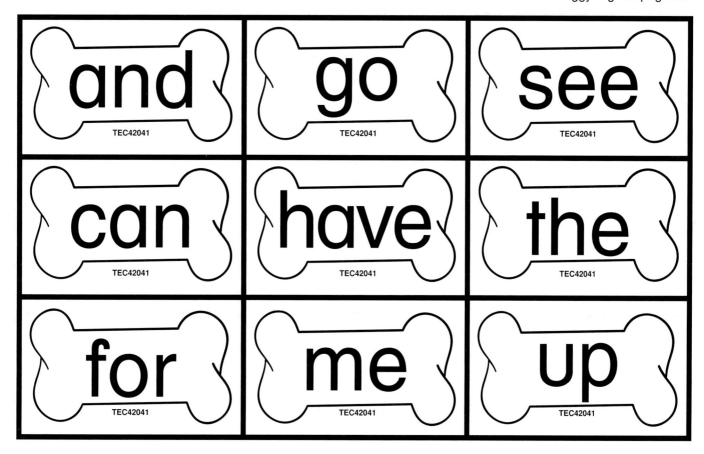

and TEC42041	**go** TEC42041	**see** TEC42041
can TEC42041	**have** TEC42041	**the** TEC42041
for TEC42041	**me** TEC42041	**up** TEC42041

Recording sheet

Name _____

Word	Tally Marks	Total
and		
can		
for		
go		
have		
me		
see		
the		
up		

©The Mailbox® · TEC42041 · Feb./Mar. 2009

Addition Cards

Use with "Ladybug Addition" on page 81.

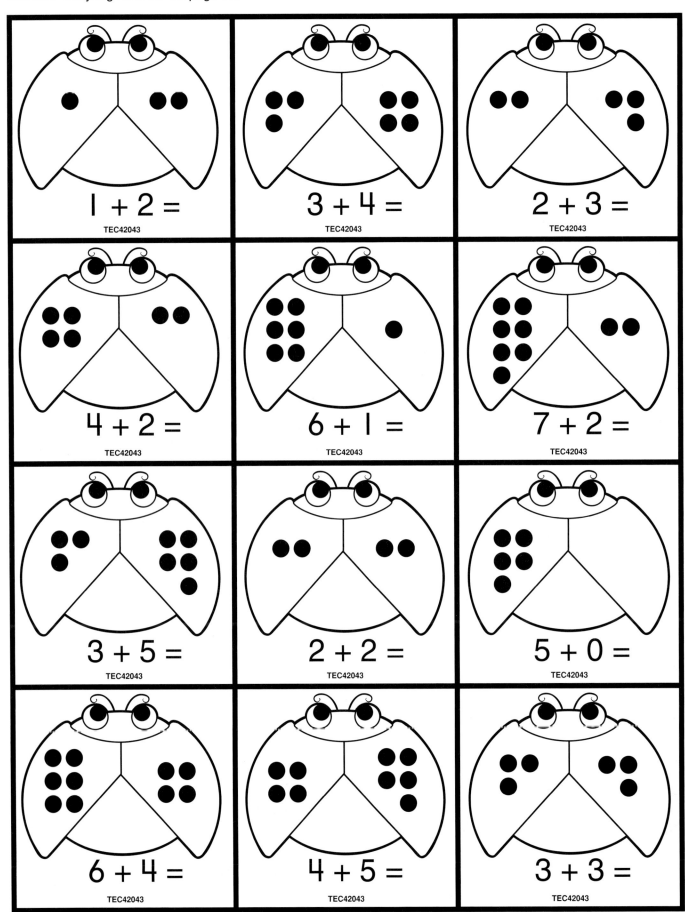

1 + 2 =
TEC42043

3 + 4 =
TEC42043

2 + 3 =
TEC42043

4 + 2 =
TEC42043

6 + 1 =
TEC42043

7 + 2 =
TEC42043

3 + 5 =
TEC42043

2 + 2 =
TEC42043

5 + 0 =
TEC42043

6 + 4 =
TEC42043

4 + 5 =
TEC42043

3 + 3 =
TEC42043

©The Mailbox® • TEC42043 • June/July 2009

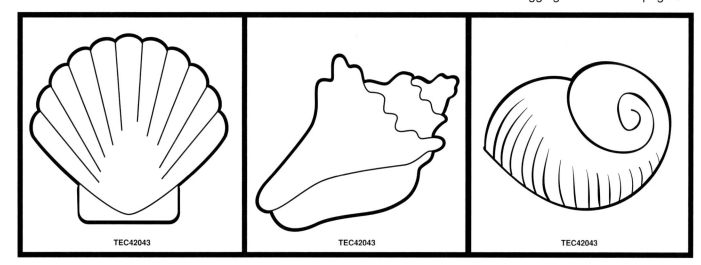

TEC42043   TEC42043   TEC42043

Name _____ Graphing

So Many Shells

 Color the graph to match the shells.

Seashells

 Write how many.

_____   _____   _____

Circle.

Which has more?

Which has fewer?

Happy Campers

Put the cards in order.
Check.

©The Mailbox® · TEC42043 · June/July 2009

Ready to Shop!

What You Need

grocery store ad

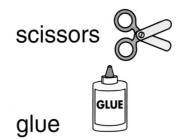

paper

scissors

glue

What You Do

(1) Cut out 4 pictures.

(2) Draw 2 lines.

(3) Glue.

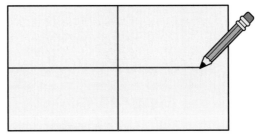

(4) Write.

apple   milk

grapes   pizza

Note to the teacher: Make a copy of this activity card and put it in a plastic page protector for durability. Then put the activity card and the needed materials at a center.

Two More!

What You Need

paper

number cube

blue crayon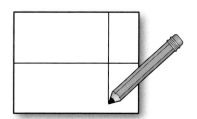

red crayon

What You Do

1. Draw 2 lines.

2. Toss. Read.

3. Draw that many ○. Write.
   blue

4. Draw two ○. Write.
   red

5. Write how many in all.

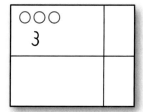

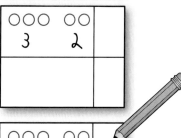

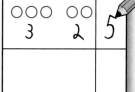

6. Do Steps 2–5 again.

Step-by-step center activity: Color a copy of this activity card and put it in a plastic page protector for durability. Then put the activity card and the needed materials at a center.

Switch!

What You Need

magnetic letters  paper

What You Do

① Write.
1.
2.
3.
4.
5.

② Make this word. **r a n**

③ Write.
1. ran
2.
3.
4.
5.

④ Change the last letter. **r a** ↙ **t**

⑤ Write.
1. ran
2. rat
3.
4.
5.

⑥ Make and write 3 more words.

©The Mailbox® • TEC42042 • April/May 2009

Step-by-step center activity: Make a copy of this activity card and put it in a plastic page protector for durability. Then put the activity card and the needed materials at a center.

LET'S DO SOCIAL STUDIES!

Let's Do Social Studies!

My World

Understanding location

To prepare, obtain five lidless boxes in different sizes. Flip the boxes upside down and label them as shown, leaving the smallest box blank. Hold up a card with a youngster's name and street address and say, "[Student's name] lives at [street address]." Place the card on the smallest box. Place the next largest box over the smaller box and say, "[Her] street is in [city's name]." Continue saying the name of each location until all of the boxes have been placed beneath the box labeled "Earth." On each of several days, repeat the activity with each child's address, prompting youngsters to supply the information and move the boxes.

Mary Davis
Keokuk Christian Academy
Keokuk, IA

Community Connection

Awareness of goods and services

Help students see that goods and services exist in their communities with this picture-perfect booklet! Take photographs of local businesses and the people who work there. (Be sure to obtain permission first.) Then arrange the photos in a small album. Share the album with the class and have students help write captions for each page; then display the booklet in your class library.

This is Harper's Bakery. Bobby's mom is the baker. Lindsay's birthday cake came from Harper's. The bakery provides goods like cakes and cookies.

Let's Do Social Studies!

In Tune With George Washington

Recognizing Presidents' Day

Invite your little ones to march in place as you lead them in singing this song about George Washington. For a home–school connection, give each child a copy of the song card on page 102 to sing with a family member.

(sung to the tune of "When the Saints Go Marching In")

George Washington,
George Washington,
First president of this great land.
He is the "Father of Our Country."
Hip, hip, hooray for Washington!

George Washington,
George Washington,
He led the soldiers in the war.
He helped to earn our country's freedom.
Hip, hip, hooray for Washington!

adapted from an idea by Karen Potter
Red Oak-Sturgeon Elementary
Alberta, VA

A Great Idea!

Recognizing Black History Month

Highlight contributions of notable black inventors with this fact-filled poem.

An inventor is someone
Who creates something new.
It makes our lives better
And easier too!

Benjamin Banneker made a clock that was new.
W. A. Deitz designed a new shoe.
Mr. Latimer invented a better kind of light.
Sarah Goode made a bed that folded just right!

adapted from an idea by Deborah Garmon
Groton, CT

Where I Live

Comparing locations of places

This art project helps kindergartners understand the size correlation between house, street, city, and state. In advance, fold a sheet of 12" x 18" white construction paper in half three times, as shown, for each child. Have the child position the resulting booklet horizontally (with the fold at the top) and draw a picture of her house. Then have her open the booklet once and turn it horizontally again, this time drawing a picture of the street she lives on. Have her repeat the process twice more, drawing the city she lives in and then the state. Help her label each picture appropriately.

Melinda Blackwill, Hays, KS

Let's Do Social Studies!

Marvelous Maps

Identifying uses for maps

Display a world map, a street map, and a map of a mall or other building. Lead students in singing several rounds of the song shown. Then ask youngsters to look at the maps and describe why people might need each one. For example, a world map can be used to find the name of a country, a street map can help with driving directions, and a mall map can help a person who is trying to find a restroom.

(sung to the tune of "Mary Had a Little Lamb")

Maps can help us find our way,
Find our way every day.
Maps can help us find our way
Wherever we may go.

Michelle Ferraro, Ashley Mason, Theresa Mullican,
   Laura Rider, Aimee Speary
Bester Elementary
Hagerstown, MD

Can Collection

Citizenship: responsibility

Spotlight respecting the earth with a variety of skill-based recycling activities! Encourage students' families to send in clean aluminum drink cans and then engage youngsters in one or more of the activities below. When the activities are complete, have students help you place the cans in a recycling bin or take them to a recycling facility.

- Count the cans and place them in groups of ten.
- Sort the cans by soda type and make a graph.
- Remove the can tabs and spray-paint them. When they're dry, use the tabs for patterning activities.

Sandie Bolze
Verne W. Critz Elementary
East Patchogue, NY

Find the Animal

Reading a map

Have youngsters help you create a simple map of your classroom. Laminate the map. Then direct a student to stand just outside your classroom door while a second child places a stuffed animal toy somewhere in the classroom. Have a third youngster use a dry-erase marker to draw a line on the map from the door to the animal. Then invite the first child into the room and give her the map. Encourage her to follow the path on the map to find the toy!

Nancy Carpenter
Paw Creek Elementary
Charlotte, NC

Let's Do Social Studies!

We Care

Recognizing ways to protect Earth's resources

Promote student awareness about protecting Earth's air, land, and water with this idea. Have each child place a damp coffee filter at the top of a sheet of white construction paper. Then invite him to paint the filter with green and blue watercolors to look like Earth. Remind students that Earth contains more water than land, so they should paint more blue than green. After removing the filter to reveal the earth painting on the paper, allow the paper to dry. To complete the project, ask each youngster to dictate a sentence about how he can help take care of Earth. Write the sentence along the bottom of his paper.

Nicole Bunting
Parkview Elementary
Columbia, IL

I will not throw trash in the lake.
Roger

Ode to America

Exposure to maps

Prior to leading students in singing this song, display a United States map. Point to the states mentioned as the class sings. After repeating the song several times, invite volunteers to point to the states on the map. If desired, replace the states in the song with others to provide more practice with map skills.

(sung to the tune of "O Christmas Tree")

America, America,
We love the USA.
America, America,
The country with 50 states
From Florida to Washington,
From California to Michigan.
America, America,
We love the USA.

Amy Ryan
Grace Lutheran School
St. Petersburg, FL

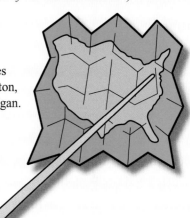

Goods

cookies
clothes
toys
pizza
video games

Services

giving a haircut
filling a cavity
cleaning a house

Who Made It?

Goods and services

This activity helps youngsters understand the differences between goods and services. In advance draw a hand on a large sheet of paper. Title the paper and another sheet of paper as shown. To begin, explain that goods are items we want that can be touched or used. Then explain that services are things we want that others do for us; services do not always have a final product that can be touched. Enlist students' help in compiling a list on each poster. Then display the posters as a nifty reminder of the differences between goods and services.

Song Cards

Use with "In Tune With George Washington" on page 99.

In Tune With George Washington ♪

(sung to the tune of "When the Saints Go Marching In")

George Washington,
George Washington,
First president of this great land.
He is the "Father of Our Country."
Hip, hip, hooray for Washington!

George Washington,
George Washington,
He led the soldiers in the war.
He helped to earn our country's freedom.
Hip, hip, hooray for Washington!

©The Mailbox • February/March 2009

In Tune With George Washington ♪

(sung to the tune of "When the Saints Go Marching In")

George Washington,
George Washington,
First president of this great land.
He is the "Father of Our Country."
Hip, hip, hooray for Washington!

George Washington,
George Washington,
He led the soldiers in the war.
He helped to earn our country's freedom.
Hip, hip, hooray for Washington!

©The Mailbox • February/March 2009

MANAGEMENT TIPS & TIMESAVERS

Management Tips & Timesavers

Messages and Reminders

Make lost parent notes a thing of the past! For each child, make a blank booklet for home-school communication. Put the booklet in a personalized pocket folder in which you have fastened a top-loading page protector. Encourage each youngster to take his folder home daily and return it to school the next day. Whenever you write a note to a child's parents, alert them by putting the booklet in the page protector and have them do likewise when they write to you. If you need to give the whole class the same message, simply print the message on adhesive labels and place a label in each journal. *Michelle Morrow, Red Bank Elementary, Lexington, SC*

Handy for Helpers

For each classroom job, glue a corresponding labeled photo or picture to an individual library pocket. (See the picture cards on page 110.) Display the pockets as desired. Then put a personalized craft stick in each pocket to assign the jobs. To reassign the duties, just move the sticks to different pockets! *Katherine Boldt, McKinley Elementary, Appleton, WI*

Library Helper

"A-peel-ing" Behavior

Here's a fresh approach to encouraging positive behavior! Trace a large apple cutout on a paper-backed bulletin board. Then draw a leaf and stem. Next, visually divide the back of the cutout into several sections and number them sequentially. Then cut apart the sections. Whenever students exhibit exceptionally good behavior, post an apple section on the board so the pieces are displayed in order. After the entire apple is assembled, reward the students as desired. *Heather E. Graley, Grace Christian School, Blacklick, OH*

Hands, Feet, and More!

This call-and-response chant helps students line up quickly.

Teacher: Hands
Students: Back   (*Put hands behind backs.*)

Teacher: Feet
Students: Together   (*Put feet together.*)

Teacher: Face
Students: Forward   (*Face the front.*)

Teacher: Mouth
Students: Mmm   (*Stop talking.*)

Aubrey Brinkmeyer, West End Elementary, Industry, TX

Personal Space

To help each student stay in his own area during floor activities, have youngsters sit on inexpensive vinyl placemats. The placemats clearly define each youngster's space. Plus, they're easy to clean and require little storage space. For added kid appeal, use different placemats throughout the year to correspond with topics of study or the seasons. *Jennifer Weinstein, Trumansburg Elementary, Trumansburg, NY*

Management Tips & Timesavers

Pleasing Paper Storage

For quick and easy access to different colors of construction paper, label a separate hanging file folder for each color. Store the paper in the appropriate folders in a file cabinet or crate. The paper will stay in good condition, and you'll have the colors you need at your fingertips! *Anna N. Morris, L. B. J. Elementary, Jackson, KY*

Purple

Mess-Free Painting

Cleaning paint cups is a snap with this idea! Before you pour paint into a paint cup, place a small resealable plastic bag in the cup and then turn the top of the bag over the edge of the cup. When it's time to clean the cup, simply remove the bag and throw it away. Or, if you want to save unused paint, seal the bag for later use. Either way, you won't have messy paint cups! *adapted from an idea by Laura Boeve, Beverly Elementary, Beverly Hills, MI*

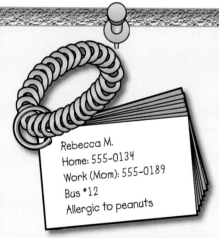

Rebecca M.
Home: 555-0134
Work (Mom): 555-0189
Bus #12
Allergic to peanuts

Ready for Emergencies

To keep students' emergency information close at hand, list each child's contact, transportation, and pertinent health information on a separate blank card. Punch a hole in each card and secure the cards on a coil key ring. Keep the key ring near your classroom door. Whenever you and your students leave the room, slip the key ring on your wrist. If there is a fire drill or an emergency when you're away from the room, you'll have the information you need! *Karen Potter, Red Oak-Sturgeon Elementary, Alberta, VA*

Space Dividers

If your students have difficulty staying in their own table space, divide the tops of the tables with colorful electrical tape. The tape clearly defines each student's work area. Plus, if you use different-colored tape for each table, you can identify each group by color! *Laura Chapman, Chapel Glen Elementary, Indianapolis, IN*

Picture Perfect

With this tip, even young students can keep classroom supplies neat and organized! In each classroom area in which students use materials independently, post a photo that shows how the area should look. If desired, color-code the supplies and the shelves or containers where they belong. Not only will students know where to return the supplies, but they will also know how to arrange them! *Melissa Rent, Stonegate Elementary, Zionsville, IN*

Management Tips & Timesavers

A Frosty Friend

This wintertime pal promotes positive behavior. Display a snowpal cutout on a classroom wall and place glue and cotton balls nearby. Each time the class exhibits exceptionally good behavior, glue a cotton ball to the snowpal. When a predetermined number of cotton balls are on the snowpal, reward students with a special treat or privilege. *Judi Lesnansky, New Hope Academy, Youngstown, OH*

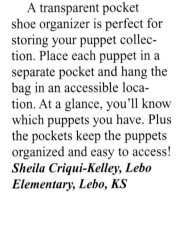

Pockets of Puppets

A transparent pocket shoe organizer is perfect for storing your puppet collection. Place each puppet in a separate pocket and hang the bag in an accessible location. At a glance, you'll know which puppets you have. Plus the pockets keep the puppets organized and easy to access! *Sheila Criqui-Kelley, Lebo Elementary, Lebo, KS*

Places for Pieces

When it's time for cut-and-glue projects, give each child a personalized gallon-size resealable plastic bag. The child cuts out the necessary pieces and then places them in his bag for safekeeping until it's time to glue them. No more lost pieces! *Paula Haines, Arcadia Public School, Arcadia, WI*

The Zero Zone

Help students stay quiet in the hallways with this simple suggestion. Once youngsters are lined up, have each child make a zero with his thumb and forefinger. Then remind little ones that zero means nothing or none. Explain that the hallway is the Zero Zone and there is no talking. If a student needs a reminder when you're in the hallway, simply show him the zero symbol. *Monica Yankus, St. John the Baptist Catholic School, Plattsmouth, NE*

Double-Duty Folders

Try this twist on traditional take-home folders to keep important information handy. Use clear packing tape to attach copies of desired information— such as class schedules, a class list, sight words, and teacher-contact information—to the front of a two-pocket folder. The information will be easily accessible to parents and students, and it will be less likely to get lost! *Fawn Wessel, Madison Elementary, Gardner, KS*

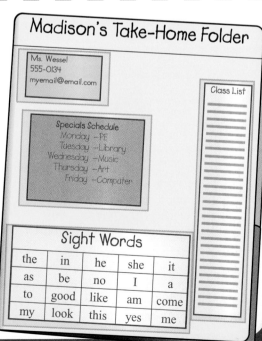

Management Tips & Timesavers

Sturdy Hall Passes

Unwanted CDs make perfect hall passes. Use a permanent marker to label the blank side of each CD as a hall pass. Tie a yarn loop through the middle of the CD and hang it near the door. When a youngster leaves the room, she takes a hall pass and then hangs it back up when she returns. *Emile Blake, Tuttle Elementary, Maiden, NC*

Hall Pass

Ms. Blake
Grade K

Organized Letters

Here's an easy way to organize your letter manipulatives. Label each pocket of a transparent shoe organizer with two or three different letters and then sort the manipulatives into the corresponding pockets. Hang the organizer in an accessible location and invite youngsters to take manipulatives as needed. *Emily McCann, Darby Woods Elementary, Galloway, OH*

Crisscross Applesauce

This simple sign provides a nonverbal reminder. To make a sign, glue the label from an applesauce jar to a piece of tagboard. Then tape a jumbo craft stick to the back of the tagboard. When students are sitting on the floor for group time, remind them to sit with their legs crossed in front of them (in crisscross applesauce–style) by simply holding up the sign. *Lisa Carlson, Ridge Hill Elementary, Hamden, CT*

Don't Forget!

If your students often leave items behind at the end of the day, try this! Add either Cubby Patrol or Coat Hook Checker to your classroom job chart. After students have gathered their belongings, the assigned youngster checks the cubbies or coat hook area and returns left-behind items to the appropriate students. If he is unsure about an item's owner, he displays it for the group. *Jen Goldman, Sol Feinstone Elementary, Newtown, PA*

Magnetic Organizers

Make piles of jumbled materials a thing of the past! Sort supplies—such as paper clips, brad fasteners, rubber bands, pens, and erasers—into separate resealable plastic bags. Seal the bags and adhere a strip of magnetic tape to the back of each. Attach the bags to a magnetic surface, such as a filing cabinet or a whiteboard. You'll be able to locate materials in an instant! *Heather E. Graley, Grace Christian School, Blacklick, OH*

Management Tips & Timesavers

A Full Basket

Promote positive behavior with this "eggs-tra" special display. Post an Easter basket cutout. Each time your students exhibit especially good behavior, attach an egg cutout to the basket. When a predetermined number of eggs have been added to the basket, reward the class as desired. For added fun, use a real basket and a supply of plastic eggs.

Seating Setup

This simple seating chart can be easily updated and doubles as a valuable substitute teacher tool. Write each child's name on a small sticky note and arrange the notes on a sheet of paper to match the seating arrangement in your classroom. Then tuck the handy reference into a page protector. When a child's seat changes, simply rearrange the appropriate sticky note. *Pamela Figueiredo, United Christian School, Garden City, MI*

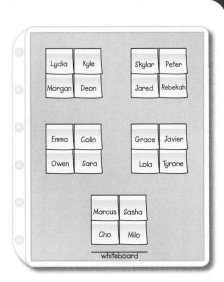

Two by Two

To pair students for partner activities or games, give each child a card programmed with an uppercase or a lowercase letter. (Be sure each card you distribute has a match.) Have each youngster locate her partner by finding the child with the matching card. *Kelly Liston, Northwood Academy Charter School, Philadelphia, PA*

Restroom Roundup

Lead your students in this catchy song while lining up for the restroom. It's full of helpful reminders!

(sung to the tune of "Where Is Thumbkin?")

Time for the restroom.
Time for the restroom.
Please, line up.
Please, line up.
Wash your hands with water.
Don't forget the soap!
Please, don't talk.
Remember to walk!

Katie Klipp
Bob Jones Elementary
Greenville, SC

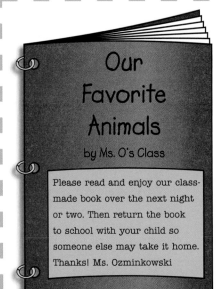

Our Favorite Animals
by Ms. O's Class

Please read and enjoy our class-made book over the next night or two. Then return the book to school with your child so someone else may take it home. Thanks! Ms. Ozminkowski

Bright Reminders

To encourage parents to return borrowed class-made books, try this! Attach a brightly colored copy of a reminder, such as the one shown, to each book your class makes. The easy-to-see message will prompt parents to return the books in a timely manner. *Barbara Ozminkowski, Mary Helen Guest Elementary, Walled Lake, MI*

Management Tips & Timesavers

"Co-pop-eration"!

Your class will pop over this delicious cooperation-building display! Post a large cutout of a popcorn box on a bulletin board. Prepare a supply of popped kernel cutouts and store them in an accessible location. When you notice students working well together, write your observation on a popcorn piece and staple it above the box. Once the board accumulates a set number of popcorn pieces, reward your class with a special treat or privilege.

Jake and Allie shared glue at center time!

Popcorn

Ready-to-Go Bingo

Distribute bingo materials in no time with this organizational tip. For each child, place a game card and a sufficient number of counters in a large resealable plastic bag. When it's time to play, simply give each child a bag. Instruct her to keep the counters in her bag and remove each one as needed. After the game, have each child place her card and counters back in the bag for the next game. *Kathi Carter, Greene County Tech Primary, Paragould, AR*

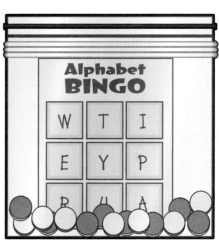

Alphabet BINGO

| W | T | I |
| E | Y | P |

You've Got Mail!

Have a deskful of students' masterpieces drawn just for you? Here's an easy way to keep your desk organized while honoring those little treasures. Purchase an inexpensive plastic mailbox from a home improvement store. Write your name on the side with a permanent marker and set the mailbox on a shelf near your desk. When students have special deliveries, ask them to place their drawings in your mailbox so you can enjoy the pictures at the end of the day. *Teresa Richardson, Clover Garden Charter School, Burlington, NC*

Permission Pet

Use a small stuffed animal to help students learn the importance of raising their hands and taking turns to talk. Select a stuffed animal to be the class's permission pet. After asking a question, toss the pet to the student who raises his hand first, giving him permission to speak. After the child shares, have him toss the pet back to you. In no time, the permission pet will encourage students to take turns! *Melissa Fletcher, Central Catholic Elementary, Du Bois, PA*

Mobile Bulletin Boards

Easily change your bulletin boards and create extra display space with trifold boards. Decorate one board for each theme you teach. As classroom themes change, simply store the old board and replace it with a new one. To reuse a trifold board, attach cutouts with rubber cement so you can easily remove them. *Mary Amoson, Moreland Elementary, Moreland, GA*

Animals and Their Babies

Picture Cards

Use with "Handy for Helpers" on page 104.

Line Leader TEC42038	**Door Holder** TEC42038	**Messenger** TEC42038
Boys' Bathroom Monitor TEC42038	**Girls' Bathroom Monitor** TEC42038	**Library Helper** TEC42038
Chair Helper TEC42038	**Paper Passer** TEC42038	**Supply Helper** TEC42038
Snack Helper TEC42038	**Lunch Helper** TEC42038	**Trash Helper** TEC42038

OUR READERS WRITE

Our Readers Write

Picture This!

Here's a kid-pleasing way to introduce yourself to students. Gather a few photos of yourself from when you were about their age. Then display the photos as desired in a prominent classroom location. No doubt youngsters will enjoy seeing that you were once a student just like them!

Mary Beth Pugh
Vance Elementary
Vance, AL

Ms. Pugh

Me!

My First Day of School

My Class

Glue Guidance

To help students use an appropriate amount of glue on projects, I teach them this simple rhyme.

How Much?
Just a little glue will do.
Just a dot, not a lot.

Ina Austin
W. G. Mallet School
Farmington, ME

James

Pleasing Portfolios

On the first day of school, I have each student draw an illustration on the front of a personalized file folder. Then I collect the folders. Every month I have each youngster choose a sample of his best work for me to put in his folder. At the end of the school year, I return each student's folder and ask him to draw an illustration on the back of it. When students compare their two illustrations and review their work samples, they're sure to be amazed by the progress they made!

Susan Schipper
Charles Street School
Palmyra, NJ

Seasonal Center Signs

My center signs double as classroom decorations. I make large seasonal cutouts and laminate them for durability. For example, I make apples in the fall, snowpals in the winter, and flowers in the spring. I suspend each sign above the corresponding center or supply area. They make my classroom bright and cheery!

Jennifer Farneski, Watsessing School
Bloomfield, NJ

MATH CENTER

Our Readers Write

Wonderful Weavings

During our spider unit, I tell my students about different types of webs, such as orb, triangular, flat, and tangled webs. Then I have each youngster use rubber bands and a Geoboard to make a model of a web we learned about or a web of his own creation. It gives students a new appreciation for nature!

Kelly Finch
Vaughan Elementary
Powder Springs, GA

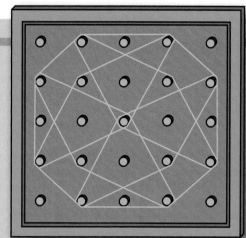

For Parents

Before fall parent-teacher conferences, I showcase on a hallway wall photographs of classroom activities, field trips, and special school events. Then I post captions on leaf cutouts. The display is easy to prepare and it's an excellent way to show parents what their children have been doing at school. After I take the display down, I save the photos in a class scrapbook or send them home with students.

Emily Ryherd
Helen Baker Elementary
Glencoe, MN

Turkey Tune

Here's a cute song that's perfect for a Thanksgiving performance.

(sung to the tune of "I'm a Little Teapot")

I'm a little turkey,   *(Place hands on hips.)*
Short and fat.

Here on the farm   *(Point down.)*
Is where I've sat.

When it's near   *(Cup hands
Thanksgiving,   around mouth.)*
Hear me shout,

"Open the gate   *(Swing arm out.)*
And let me out!"

Stephanie Ives
Deep Springs Elementary
Lexington, KY

Seasonal Reading Sticks

After my colleagues or I make seasonal cut-outs with a die-cut machine, I laminate several castoffs. Then I attach each castoff to a separate ruler to make reading sticks. My students and I use the sticks to frame letters, numbers, and sight words. Youngsters also use the sticks when they "read" the room!

Linda Tavares
Clara Macy Elementary
Bellingham, MA

Our Readers Write

Mystery Readers

I build students' anticipation for storytime with the help of surprise guest readers. Each Friday I have a student's parent, a school staff member, a high school student, or a community worker visit my class and read aloud a chosen book. Some weeks I invite people associated with current topics of study. For example, during Fire Prevention Week, I arrange for a firefighter to be our guest. I put the featured books in our classroom library and they quickly become class favorites!

Casey Cooksey, Bruce Elementary, Bruce, MS

Watch the Road!

To help students improve their cutting skills, I encourage each youngster to imagine her scissors are a car, she is the driver, and the cutting line is the road. I tell her to "drive" carefully and not to speed so her car stays on the road. Students love this analogy and it's easy for them to remember!

Cheryl Hatcher, New Concord Elementary
New Concord, OH

Daily Recap

A puppet helps my students remember what we learned each day. A short time before dismissal, I "wake up" a nocturnal animal puppet. Since the puppet was "sleeping" during the day, I invite youngsters to tell the puppet about the day's activities. It keeps our dismissal time calm. Plus, when students go home, they're ready to tell their families about the day!

Devany Marino
Londonderry Elementary
Middletown, PA

Friendly Fishing

For character education, I write on each of several fish cutouts (patterns on page 122) a word that describes a positive or negative character trait. I attach a paper clip to each fish and then spread out the fish facedown on the floor. Students take turns "catching" the fish with a magnetic fishing pole. Whenever a student "catches" a fish, we discuss whether the corresponding word describes a good friend and then sort the fish accordingly. It's a terrific way to promote positive behavior!

Kathy Sharp
Kingston Elementary
Berea, KY

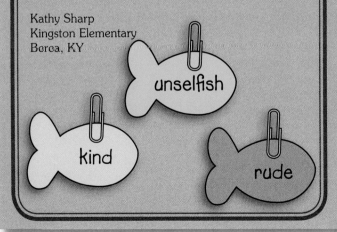

"Sense-ational" Holders

Inexpensive salt and pepper shakers are great supplies for a five senses unit! I use opaque shakers or line clear shakers with colored paper to keep the contents of the shakers secret. I put something with a different scent in each shaker. To save the prepared shakers for reuse, I simply seal the tops of them with plastic wrap.

Katherine Gegner
Linkhorne Elementary
Lynchburg, VA

Our Readers Write

Sing a Seasonal Song

To add toe-tapping fun to our December and January calendar time, I have my youngsters sing each song shown during the appropriate month. I copy the songs on chart paper so students can follow along.

(sung to the tune of "The Farmer in the Dell")

December is now here.
We're spreading lots of cheer.
Christmas, Kwanzaa, Hanukkah,
December is now here.

The last month of the year,
The last month of the year.
December is the last of twelve,
The last month of the year.

(sung to the tune of "Twinkle, Twinkle, Little Star")

J-A-N-U-A-R-Y,
Time to tell the old year, "Bye."
Snowmen, mittens, cold winds blow.
It's the first month, we all know.
J-A-N-U-A-R-Y
2009, let's all say, "Hi!"

Cheryl Bristol, Jenkins Elementary, Hickory, NC

Cheery Christmas Reindeer

Looking for a festive holiday art project? It's right in your students' hands! Each student uses brown paint to make handprints (without painting the thumb) on his paper. After the paint is dry, he decorates the picture with buttons, ribbons, and other craft materials.

Kelly Kramer, Rivercrest Elementary, Bartlett, TN

A Basketful of Buddies

Children in my class who hesitate to read to another child love the idea of reading to a stuffed toy reading buddy. I place a collection of stuffed toys in a basket. Then I encourage youngsters to sit down with a chosen toy and a book.

Heather Minter
Meadville Elementary
Nathalie, VA

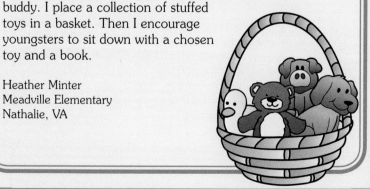

Watchful Pencil

To motivate my students to do their best work, I invite one student each day to use my Watchful Pencil. To make one, I glue a wiggle eye on the unsharpened end of a pencil. When I give the pencil to a child, I tell him he can use my pencil that day so it can watch him do his best work.

Cindy Johnson
West-Yadkin Elementary
Hamptonville, NC

Our Readers Write

A Humorous Holiday

When holiday items go on sale, I begin preparing for a special April Fool's Day joke. I purchase small objects such as Halloween stickers, Christmas pencils, Valentine's Day candy, and St. Patrick's Day beads. Then I wrap assorted items together in small packages. Before my students arrive on April Fool's Day, I put one package on each child's desk. My students are delighted to open the packages and find the mixed-up holiday gifts!

Amy Hart, Saint Sylvester School, Pittsburgh, PA

Spin and Ask!

I use this simple game to promote conversation skills. To prepare, I partially fill a bottle with sand. Then I glue a smiley face on the bottom of the bottle. Once students are seated in a circle, I lay the bottle on its side in the middle of the circle and spin it. When it stops, the child who is facing the smiley face asks a question of the child to whom the bottle is pointing. The second child answers the question. This activity is especially meaningful for my English language learners.

Ruby Treviòo
Instituto San Roberto, Garza Garcia
Nuevo León, Mexico

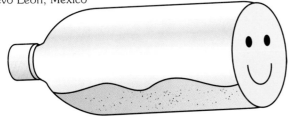

Check Your Spacing

To remind my students to leave a space between words, we sing this song before each writing lesson.

(sung to the tune of "Are You Sleeping?")

Check your spacing.
Check your spacing.
Between words,
Between words.
Mark it with two fingers.
Mark it with two fingers
To help you,
To help you.

Cami Zook
Eagle Elementary
Brownsburg, IN

Holiday Gifts

For a simple gift for each student, I place in a resealable plastic bag a ball of homemade play dough. (See the recipe on the right.) Then I send the bag home with a cookie cutter, the dough recipe, and several developmentally appropriate suggestions for playing with the dough, such as forming letters, words, shapes, and numbers.

Alesia Richards
Redbud Run Elementary
Winchester, VA

Homemade Play Dough

1 c. flour
½ c. salt
2 tsp. cream of tartar
1 c. water
1 tsp. vegetable oil
food coloring

Mix the dry ingredients. Then add the remaining ingredients and stir. In a heavy skillet, cook the mixture for two to three minutes, stirring frequently. Knead the dough until it becomes soft and smooth. Store the dough in an icing tub.

Our Readers Write

Entertaining Erasers

Looking for a fun way to motivate students to practice blending sounds? Invite youngsters to design silly sock erasers! Each child uses markers and other art supplies to create a funny face on an old white tube sock. As I call out sounds, each youngster writes the corresponding letters on his board. Wearing their silly sock erasers on their nonwriting hands, students are eager to wipe their boards clean and try again!

Deborah Provencher
West Brookfield Elementary
West Brookfield, MA

Rainbow Parfait

This tasty St. Patrick's Day treat doubles as a delicious way to practice colors! In advance, I ask each student to bring two cups of chopped fruit in an assigned rainbow color, such as red strawberries or green kiwi slices. To make the snack, a child layers fruit in a clear cup with each layer representing a color of the rainbow. She tops her edible rainbow with whipped cream and a sprinkle of golden raisins (to represent gold at the end of the rainbow). Then I take pictures of each child with her treat. The following day, she uses her picture to write a how-to piece describing the steps.

Colleen Thursam
Tenniswood Elementary
Clinton Township, MI

Handy Hearts

For tracers that are both practical and durable, I save heart-shaped valentine candy boxes. I keep a supply handy in my art center for my kindergartners to trace when making Valentine's Day projects.

Diane Adams, Nashua Child Learning Center, Nashua, NH

Worksheet Extenders

Here's an easy way to provide differentiation for students. First, I copy a regular-size worksheet onto legal-size paper. Then I add additional directions as shown. Finally, I simply make copies for those students who need enrichment in the selected skill.

Alexis Markis, Justice Street School, West Hills, CA

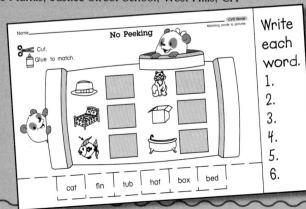

Our Readers Write

Magnetic Math

I discovered that colorful plastic milk jug lids make marvelous math counters! I ask parents to send in lids throughout the year. Once I have a supply, I stick an adhesive magnet to each lid and store the lids in a container near my magnetic whiteboard. Students enjoy using the lids for counting, patterning, and graphing activities. What a colorful way to count!

Deborah Provencher
West Brookfield Elementary
West Brookfield, MA

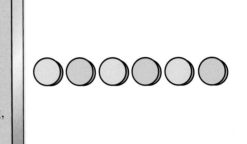

Mother's Day Garden

Before Mother's Day, I have youngsters plant a variety of grass, bean, and wildflower seeds in biodegradable peat pots. I also ask a fast-food restaurant to donate a class set of sectioned cardboard drink holders with handles. The students decorate the outsides of their holders with drawings of insects, butterflies, worms, and grass. We place crumpled tissue paper in each section and set each plant inside. Then my youngsters make thumbprint ladybugs and butterflies, cut them out, glue them onto craft sticks, and press them into the soil. Each child has a portable take-home garden to give to his mother or other special friend!

Mary Reyes
James B. Havard Elementary
Houston, TX

Flash Card Fun

To add a silly twist with math or vocabulary flash cards, I invite youngsters to call out their answers using a variety of voices. I may ask them to answer in a tiny voice, a deep voice, or even a big, bad wolf voice. No matter what voice is used, it always sounds like fun!

Annette Hamill
Collins Elementary
Collins, MS

Puppet Pointers

When I need a surefire way to grab my students' attention, I pull out one of my cute puppet pointers! To make each one, I insert a three-foot-long wooden dowel into a cloth finger puppet, stuff it with polyester filling, and hot-glue the bottom of the puppet to seal it to the stick. Youngsters love seeing which puppet pointer will help me introduce a new lesson!

Teresa Richardson
Clover Garden Charter School
Burlington, NC

Our Readers Write

Sing and Read

To motivate students to read, I create a reproducible sheet for each of our morning songs. I use an easy-to-read font and replace one or two words in each song with a blank. Each child is given a different song sheet and is invited to read the song, fill in the missing words (with help), and draw a picture to go along with the lyrics. The pages are collected and bound into a class book which we use each morning as we sing. Students love seeing their own artwork accompanying the songs!

Christina Travers
Little River Elementary
Orlando, FL

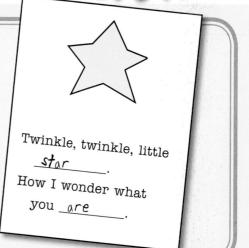

Twinkle, twinkle, little
star.
How I wonder what
you _are_.

Word Families on the Go

Word family labels on student tables are a fun way for my youngsters to practice blending words. As I call students to transition from one activity to another, I give each child a letter. The child orally blends her letter with her table's word family and says the word as she moves to a new activity. Every few days, I change each table's word family to allow more practice.

Jacqueline Robinson, Littleton Elementary, Cashion, AZ

Attendance Quiz

For a fun twist on taking attendance, I post a different question in my pocket chart each morning. Then I place the words *yes* and *no* at the top to head two columns. In a nearby container, I store cut sentence strips labeled with each child's name. As each student arrives, she places her name card under her answer. I have an easy-to-read attendance chart, and we have a great discussion question to begin the day!

Jennifer Schear
Clover Patch Preschool
Cedar Falls, IA

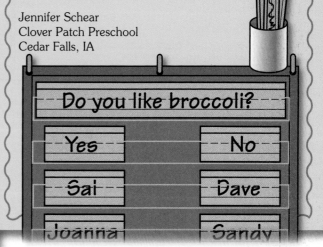

Do you like broccoli?

Yes	No
Sai	Dave
Joanna	Sandy

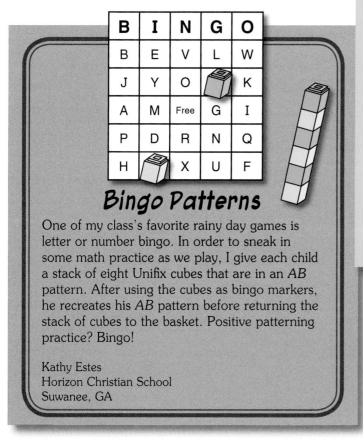

Bingo Patterns

One of my class's favorite rainy day games is letter or number bingo. In order to sneak in some math practice as we play, I give each child a stack of eight Unifix cubes that are in an *AB* pattern. After using the cubes as bingo markers, he recreates his *AB* pattern before returning the stack of cubes to the basket. Positive patterning practice? Bingo!

Kathy Estes
Horizon Christian School
Suwanee, GA

3-D Venn Diagram

To add a twist to a Venn diagram, I make a large circle by twisting together several pipe cleaners of one color. Once I have two different-colored circles, I stick them to the whiteboard to make an overlapping 3-D diagram.

Amy Rodriguez, Public School 212, Brooklyn, NY

Our Readers Write

Story Pieces

When I come across a storybook with torn or missing pages, I cut out the usable pictures of characters and other items and laminate them for durability. Then I attach pieces of adhesive-backed felt or Velcro fasteners to the backs of the items and display them on my flannelboard. My students love to manipulate the pieces to create their own stories!

Laura Thompson
Daily Discoveries
Gambrills, MD

Penpal Packs

To encourage my kindergartners to practice writing over the summer, I prepare a Penpal Pack for each child. (In advance, I obtain permission to share each child's address with her classmates.) To make a Penpal Pack, I attach a copy of the poem shown to a large resealable plastic bag. In the bag, I place a copy of a class address book, stationery, envelopes, and a pencil. I send a completed pack home with each child on the last day of school. What a great way to keep students writing and also foster lasting friendships!

adapted from an idea by Michelle Morrow
Red Bank Elementary
Lexington, SC

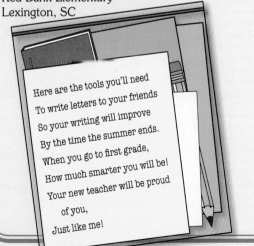

Here are the tools you'll need
To write letters to your friends
So your writing will improve
By the time the summer ends.
When you go to first grade,
How much smarter you will be!
Your new teacher will be proud
of you,
Just like me!

Campfire Songs

At the end of every school year I make a construction paper campfire and hold a class sing-along. I gather my students around the "fire," and we sing classic campfire songs and favorite songs from the school year. When we're finished singing, I provide the fixings to make s'mores as a special treat.

Roxanne Dearman
WNC Early Intervention for Deaf Children
Charlotte, NC

What Doesn't Belong?

This simple activity encourages students to use critical-thinking skills, and it is a favorite of my students! I display a poster similar to the one shown. Then I choose four cards programmed with pictures, letters, or numbers and attach them to the poster. I invite a volunteer to choose a picture he thinks doesn't belong with the other three and explain why. There are no right or wrong answers, and my students love explaining the reasoning behind their choices.

Donna Hill
Mitchell Neilson Primary
Murfreesboro, TN

What Doesn't Belong?

Our Readers Write

Manipulatives On Board

To create manipulatives for use on my magnetic whiteboard, I take photos of the manipulatives I use most often. I enlarge the photos, cut them out, and attach a piece of magnetic tape to the back of each. My manipulatives look like the ones my students are using, and they are large enough to be seen when I am demonstrating new skills on the board.

Catherine McCann
St. Stephen School
Hamden, CT

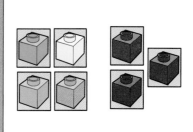

$4 + 3 = 7$

Organize for Free

When back-to-school sales begin, ask the manager of a local store if you can have the boxes that folders and notebooks are displayed in. Most stores discard the boxes when they are empty, so they may be happy to give them to you for free. The boxes are great for storing items such as take-home folders, journals, workbooks, poetry notebooks, and more!

Heather Commins
Wolfe Street Academy
Baltimore, MD

two
blue

Ready to Read

To reinforce important vocabulary, I replace the cards in my Candy Land game with cards programmed with the corresponding number and color words. My students love the added challenge of reading the words as they play this popular board game.

Jody Carlson
Smith Elementary
Berea, OH

Wearable Flags

My students are proud to wear these patriotic T-shirts. In advance, I obtain a white T-shirt for each child. I help each youngster use red fabric paint to make handprint stripes on his shirt as shown. Then I help him use blue fabric paint and a star stamper to add blue stars to the upper left corner so the design resembles the American flag.

Jill Berisford
Sherrard Elementary
Wheeling, WV

Fish Patterns
Use with "Friendly Fishing" on page 114.

SIMPLE SCIENCE

SIMPLE SCIENCE

Colorful Combinations
Making predictions, mixing colors

Getting ready:
- Set out three small clear plastic containers of water. (Baby food containers work well.)
- Gather three craft sticks or plastic spoons for stirring. Also get yellow, red, and blue food coloring.
- Make a class supply of the recording sheet on page 129.

Activity: Instruct each youngster to color the circles on her recording sheet as indicated. Next, add a drop or two of yellow food coloring to one container of water and stir it. After students observe that the water turns yellow, have them predict what will happen if you add red food coloring to the same container of water. Test their predictions. Then ask each youngster to record the results on her paper by coloring the band that connects the yellow and red circles orange. Repeat the predicting and testing process with the remaining color combinations and have students complete their papers as described.

Sue Lein
St. Jude the Apostle School
Wauwatosa, WI

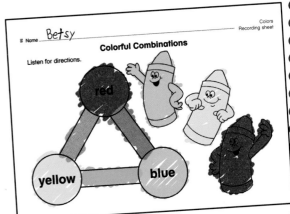

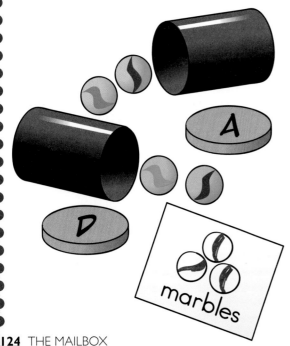

"Sound-sational" Pairs
Matching and identifying sounds

Getting ready:
- Collect ten empty black film canisters. Put in each canister pair a material or group of items that will make noise when the canister is shaken—such as soil, paper clips, or marbles—so each canister pair has the same material or items. Scramble the canisters and label each one with a different letter.
- Write the name of each different material or group of items on a separate blank card. Illustrate the cards if desired.
- Place the cards and canisters at a center.

Activity: A student shakes each canister, in turn, and pairs the canisters with like sounds. He puts each card near the pair of canisters he thinks has the corresponding contents. Then he opens the canisters and checks his work.

Carol Moynihan
Smyser Elementary
Chicago, IL

SIMPLE SCIENCE

Why Wings?
Understanding animal adaptation

Getting ready:
- Make a large two-column chart labeled as shown.
- Cut out a copy of the picture cards on page 130. Set the penguin card aside.

Activity: Present one picture card at a time and ask students whether the animal can fly; then post each picture in the matching column. Finally, display the penguin picture and ask students whether the penguin can fly. Lead children in a discussion of their ideas. Then explain that, although the penguin has wings, it cannot fly. Further explain that the penguin is an excellent swimmer. When it is underwater, it uses its wings like flippers. Post the penguin picture in the appropriate column and then display the chart as a visual reminder of this interesting animal adaptation.

Susan DeRiso
John W. Horton School
Cranston, RI

Science in Motion
Understanding the states of matter

Activity: Have each child recall experiences with water in its different states, such as ice-skating on a lake, swimming in a pool, and eating a steaming bowl of soup. Next, have each child move about the room as if he were water. Then prompt each child to move as if he were gas. Finally, have each child stand still as if he were ice.

Patricia Conner
St. Thomas More Academy
Buckeystown, MD

SIMPLE SCIENCE

Huff and Puff
Understanding that wind can move things

Getting ready:
- Stock separate stations with different lightweight items, such as writing paper, feathers, tissues, and tissue paper.
- Prepare a graph like the one shown.
- Supply a sticky note for each student.

Activity: After sharing the story *The Three Little Pigs*, remind students of the wolf's ability to knock down houses by huffing and puffing. Lead youngsters to conclude that, although they can't blow down houses like the wolf, there are some items they can move by blowing air. Display the lightweight items and invite each youngster to predict which one will be the easiest to blow into the air. Direct students to visit the stations and experiment by blowing each item. Then have each child stick a personalized note to the graph to show which object was the easiest to blow off a table. Discuss the results.

Shan Manke, Roosevelt Elementary, Detroit Lakes, MN

Easiest to Keep in the Air					
paper	Amanda				
feather	Tracey	Sal	Darryl	Geren	Sara
tissue	Dan	Karen			
tissue paper	Hunter	Heather	Jen		

The weather looks like

It is __cloudy__.

Today's temperature is __44°__ F.

Weather Watcher
Recording weather observations

Getting ready:
- Install an indoor/outdoor thermometer in your classroom.
- Use a permanent marker to program laminated poster board (or an individual whiteboard) as shown.

Activity: Select a child each day to be the Weather Watcher. Direct the youngster to draw on the whiteboard a picture of the day's weather and complete the first sentence. Then instruct him to read the thermometer and record the day's temperature. Invite the student to report his weather findings to the class. After his report, add the temperature to an ongoing class graph and erase the board to ready it for the next report.

Lindsey A. Vail, Quincy, MA

Simple Science

Chrysalis or Butterfly
Life cycle: butterfly

Getting ready:
• Obtain two colorful scarves.

Activity: Have youngsters sit in a circle. Then place the scarves (wings) in the middle of the circle. Prompt a child to walk around the circle and say, "Chrysalis," each time he touches a classmate on the head. When he touches a classmate and says, "Butterfly," have him take his classmate's seat and then encourage the newly tagged butterfly to pick up the wings and "fly" around the circle. The butterfly then begins the next round of the game.

Diane L. Flohr-Henderson
Kent City Elementary
Kent City, MI

Paper Towel Plants
Needs of living things

Getting ready:
• Place dirt in a shallow container.
• Obtain grass seeds.
• Fill a spray bottle with water.
• Make a black construction paper cone.

Activity: Have students help you spray water over the dirt until it is damp. Then encourage each child to sprinkle grass seeds in the dirt. Place the container near a sunny window. Have youngsters observe the seeds and dampen the dirt when necessary. After the seeds begin to sprout, prompt a child to place the cone over a portion of the young plants. Instruct youngsters to remove the cone after several days. Then have them share their observations, leading them to conclude that plants need sunlight to grow.

Marie E. Cecchini
West Dundee, IL

Simple Science

Good Vibrations
Investigating sound

Getting ready:
- Gather a variety of containers.
- Gather rubber bands in a variety of widths.

Activity: Gather a small group of youngsters and encourage each child to choose a container and a rubber band. Help him stretch his rubber band across his container. Then prompt him to pluck the rubber band and notice the vibrations. Write any of his observations on chart paper. Encourage him to repeat the process with a different rubber band and container. After youngsters have had several minutes to explore, read their observations aloud and add any new observations to the chart.

Diane Billman
McKitrick Elementary
Lutz, FL

Observations

The rubber bands vibrate for a long time.

When I put my hand on the rubber band, the vibration stops.

When the vibration stops, the sound stops.

Different rubber bands make different sounds.

Different containers make different sounds.

From Seed to Flower
Investigating living things

Getting ready:
- Gather a class supply of 12" x 18" blue construction paper sheets and 9" x 12" brown construction paper sheets.
- For each child, gather the following supplies: a hole-punched dot (seed), white yarn (roots), and a cupcake liner (flower).

Activity: Each student glues the brown paper to the blue paper so it resembles soil and sky. He glues the seed and roots to the soil. Next, he draws a stem and leaves in the sky and glues on a flower above the stem. To conclude, he uses his project to retell the planting and growing process to a partner. **For a more advanced version,** a child refers to a word bank to label each plant part.

Laurie Murphy
Assumption Catholic School
Bellingham, WA

Name _____

Colorful Combinations

Listen for directions.

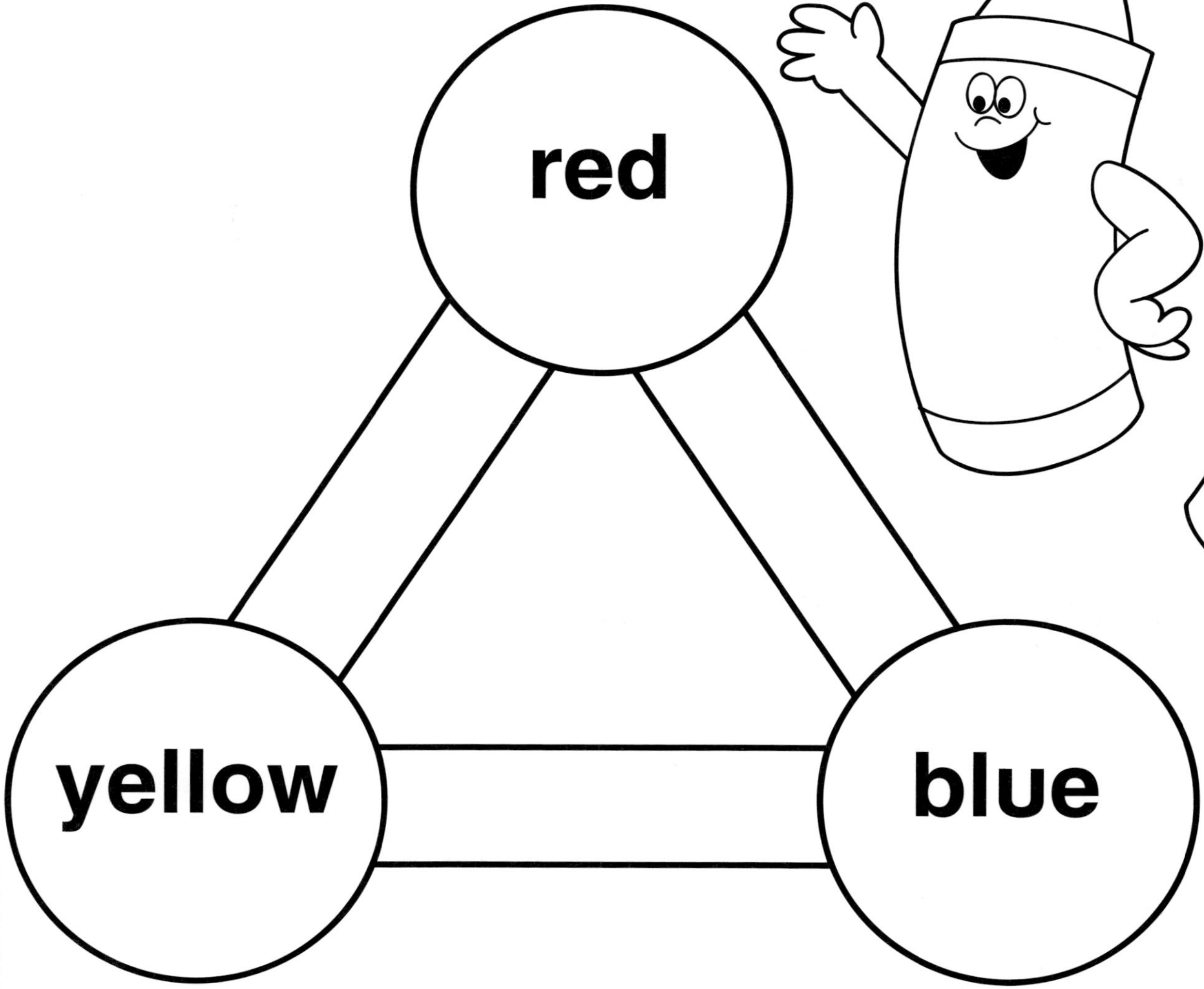

red

blue

yellow

©The Mailbox® • TEC42038 • Aug./Sept. 2008

Note to the teacher: Use with "Colorful Combinations" on page 124.

Animal Picture Cards

Use with "Why Wings?" on page 125.

butterfly

TEC42040

duck

TEC42040

bat

TEC42040

bee

TEC42040

bird

TEC42040

penguin

TEC42040

cow

TEC42040

cat

TEC42040

dog

TEC42040

mouse

TEC42040

monkey

TEC42040

horse

TEC42040

Butterfly Life Cycle Booklet

Give each child a copy of a card set from this page and a copy of the booklet pages on page 132. Have each child cut out the cards and glue them to the appropriate pages. After he cuts apart the booklet pages, help him order the pages and staple them together. Then have him read aloud each rebus sentence.

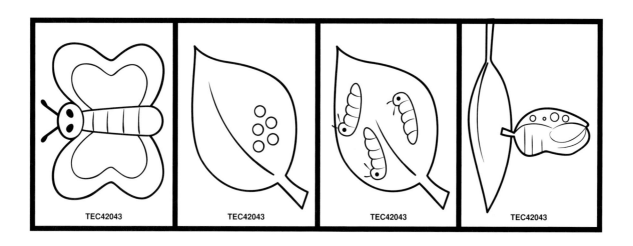

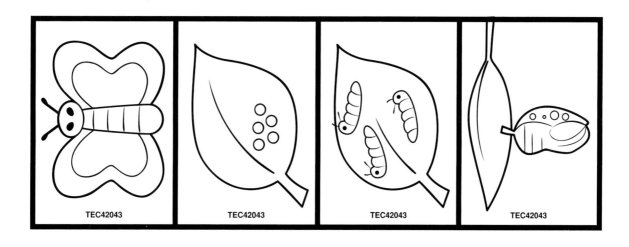

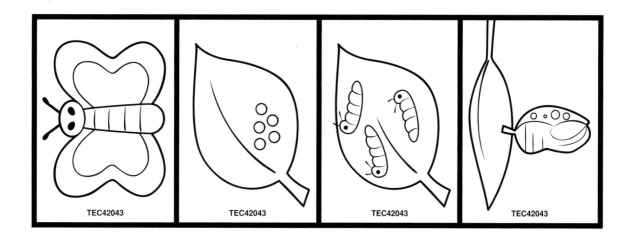

I am a [ ]. **1**

I lay [ ]. **2**

My  hatch into [ ]. **3**

Each  makes a [ ]. **4**

A  comes out of the . **5**

READING

Skills for Young Readers

Puppy Prints
Color words

Looking for a way to jump-start students' reading confidence? Try this booklet idea! Give each student one copy each of pages 146 and 147. Instruct her to write her name where indicated. Then read the cover and pages with students and have them color the illustrations to match the text. Next, ask each student to cut out the cover and booklet pages. After she sequences the pages behind the cover, staple them together. She's sure to be thrilled with the resulting booklet since she can read it on her own!

Which Letter?
Initial or final consonants

To prepare this lively game, choose whether to reinforce initial or final consonants and then post a different consonant in each of four areas of the classroom. Program a supply of blank cards with corresponding words, writing one word per card. Stack the cards facedown.

To play one round, have students stand in a circle. Play some lively music and invite students to dance or walk around the circle. After a few moments, stop the music. At this signal, each youngster goes to a posted letter. Once each child is standing near a letter, take the top word card and read it aloud without showing the word to students. Ask students to name the corresponding initial or final consonant. Have any students at the named letter sit out the next round and clap in time to the music. Then invite them to return to the game. **For a word-family variation,** post rimes and program cards with corresponding words.

adapted from an idea by Colleen Keller
Hubbard-Radcliffe Elementary
Radcliffe, IA

Mouse starts with m!

Pop and Stop!
Letter identification or high-frequency words

For this small-group review, decorate a container and a few blank cards with popcorn clip art. Make a supply of letter or word cards. Put all the cards in the container and sit with a group at a table. To take a turn, a child takes a card at random. If the card shows a letter or word, he identifies it and sets the card aside. If the card shows popcorn, he "pops" up out of his chair and returns to the container any cards that he and the other players have set aside. Then he sits back down. Students take turns as described for the allotted time.

Donna Follett, Kids Inn, Amherst, NH

Sentence or Song?
Letter-sound associations, concepts about print

Tune up several skills with this one activity! Gather five pictures whose names begin with one or more familiar letters and a card labeled "ABC." Mount the card and each picture on different sides of a small tissue box. To begin, ask a youngster to roll the box. If the box lands with a picture on top, have her name the picture, identify the corresponding initial letter, and use the word in a sentence. Write the sentence on chart paper and guide students to count the words. If the cube lands with the ABC side on top, ask students to sing the alphabet. To continue, invite a different youngster to roll the box.

Sadie Day, Carbondale Attendance Center, Carbondale, KS

Please Peek!
Word recognition

What makes these lift-the-flap books perfect for young children? They're self-checking! Choose an option below and make pages as described. (To conceal an illustration with a flap, place a paper rectangle on it and secure just the top of the rectangle.) Bind the pages between two covers and title the resulting book. After a youngster reads a page, he lifts its flap to check his reading.

Student names: Write each student's name on a separate sheet of paper and illustrate it with a corresponding photo. Conceal each photo with a flap.

Consonant-vowel-consonant words: Glue clip art for several CVC words on separate sheets of paper and write the corresponding word below each picture. Conceal each picture with a flap.

Lorena Gonzales,
Dalton Early Childhood Center, Uvalde, TX

Skills for Young Readers

Handy Lotto
High-frequency words or letter recognition

Here's a quick-and-easy game that you can use throughout the year! Have each youngster trace her hand with her fingers outstretched on a sheet of paper. List six or more high-frequency words on the board. Instruct each youngster to choose five of the words and then write each word on a different finger of her tracing. To play, name a word. Then ask each youngster with the word on her tracing to draw a colorful ring on the corresponding finger. Continue naming words and having students mark them in the same manner until one or more youngsters draws five rings and calls out, "Ring-o!" **For an easier version,** give each student a hand tracing with a different letter on each finger. Name letters for students to mark as described.

Susan McGuirl, Minue School, Carteret, NJ

Lots of Likes
Predictable text

For this class book, list on a sheet of chart paper each student's name and something he likes. (**For more advanced students,** guide each student to name something he likes that begins with the same letter as his name.) Next, give each student a sentence strip and help him write a sentence with the format shown. Instruct him to glue the sentence strip near the bottom of a large sheet of paper and then illustrate the sentence. Bind youngsters' completed papers in alphabetical order between two construction paper covers. The resulting book is a great tool for reinforcing skills such as tracking print, reading names, and alphabetical order!

Lisa Wegner
Belaire Elementary
San Angelo, TX

That Cat!
Forming -at words

This adorable feline is "purr-fect" for take-home reinforcement. Have each youngster cut out a copy of the cat pattern and letter cards on page 148. Ask her to spread out her letter cards and then form a designated -at word on her cat. After you confirm the correct spelling, name a different -at word for students to form. Continue as described until students have formed several words. Then invite each youngster to put her letters in a resealable plastic bag for easy transport home.

Sarah Lindh
Riverview Elementary, Silver Lake, WI

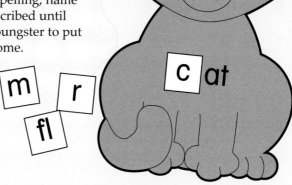

Maximizing Messages
Word recognition

Reading success is guaranteed with this ongoing idea! Use nearly the same morning message each day for a few weeks, updating information such as the weather. As students become familiar with the words in the message, incorporate the words into Concentration or lotto games. No doubt they'll soon recognize the words both in context and in isolation!

Debbie Patrick, Park Forest Elementary, State College, PA

Sounds Like Fun!
Phonological awareness

To give students practice segmenting words, have each youngster color a copy of page 149. Give him three manipulatives, such as counters, decorative glass stones, or milk jug caps. Then say a word that has one, two, or three syllables. As each youngster repeats the word, have him put one manipulative on a separate balloon for each syllable. Then ask students to identify the number of syllables. **For more advanced students**, have each youngster segment words with three sounds, placing a manipulative on a balloon as he says each sound.

Deborah Provencher
West Brookfield Elementary
West Brookfield, MA

Building Reading Skills

Take Three!

Rhyming

To prepare this three- to five-player game, color and cut out a copy of the picture cards from page 150. Mount the cards on index cards for durability. Give each player a card with a gray border. (If there are fewer than five players, set aside the extra cards with gray borders and the matching rhyming cards.) Shuffle the remaining cards and stack them facedown.

In turn, each youngster takes the top card from the stack and names the picture. If she has a matching rhyming card, she keeps the card she drew. If she does not have a matching rhyming card, she puts the card she drew in a discard pile. The players take turns, reusing the discard pile as needed, until one player has three cards.

Kathleen Poland
Tomball Elementary
Tomball, TX

Fishing Fun

Letter knowledge or word recognition

Put shredded blue paper in a plastic pool or a large plastic container so it resembles a pond. Place a plastic pail near the pond and set out a magnetic fishing pole. Make an equal number of fish cutouts in two different colors and program them using one of the options below. Staple each fish several times, putting the staples close together, and then put the fish programmed-side down in the pond. (The magnet attracts the staples.) To play, youngsters take turns fishing for matches and identifying the letters or words they catch. When a youngster gets a pair of matching fish, he puts the fish in the pail.

Letter knowledge: Program the fish of one color with uppercase letters and the remaining fish with matching lowercase letters, writing one letter per fish.

Word recognition: Writing one word per fish, write familiar words on the fish of one color and the same words on the remaining fish.

Nancy Carpenter
Silver Lake Elementary
Federal Way, WA

Grab Bag Match

Letter-sound associations

Gather several small objects. Write on the board the beginning letter of each corresponding word and then put the objects in a paper bag. (If more than one object's name has the same beginning letter, write the letter once for each object.) To begin, have a child take an object at random. Instruct her to name the object, isolate the beginning sound, and name the corresponding letter. Then ask her to circle the letter on the board and set the object aside. Continue as described until all the letters are circled. To extend the activity, have a volunteer name a displayed object and its corresponding beginning letter. Then ask him to erase the letter from the board. Continue until the board is clear.

Sandy Gabriel
West Carroll Primary School
Savanna, IL

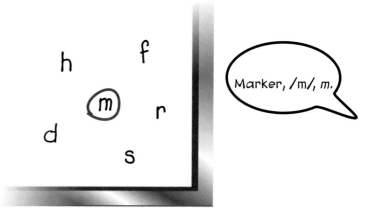

Toast and Jam

Word family: -am

For this hands-on phonics activity, draw six connected squares on a paper strip. Then write each of the following letters in a different square: b, h, j, r, S, and y. Give each child a colorful copy of the strip, a construction paper slice of toast, and a jam cutout labeled as shown. Have him glue the jam to the toast and cut apart the letters on the strip. Then name words for students to form with the rime and letters. After students successfully form each word, invite each child to use one of the words in a sentence.

Sarah Lindh
Riverview School
Silver Lake, WI

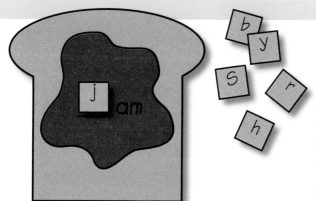

Picture-Perfect Report

Comprehension

After a child listens to a read-aloud or reads a book, give her a copy of the report form from page 151. Instruct her to write her name and the book title. Then ask her to draw and color a relevant picture in the provided space. When she is satisfied with the illustration, help her write a complete sentence about it. To keep students' interest in books high, have them complete copies of the report form throughout the year and showcase their work on a board titled "Our Book Corner."

adapted from an idea by Paula Glass
Foundations Christian Academy
Oklahoma City, OK

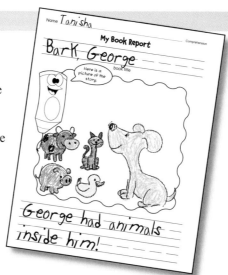

Building Reading Skills

Letters on the Bus

Letter-sound correspondence

Sing this song during circle time to help students practice naming letters and their sounds. Attach a school bus cutout to the side of an open shoebox. Gather students in a circle and place the bus in the center. Then give each child a letter card and lead the class in the song shown. At the end of the verse, the child with the matching letter places her card in the bus. Repeat the song for each card, changing the sound and last word accordingly.

(sung to the tune of "The Wheels on the Bus")

The *[A]* on the bus goes
[/a/, /a/, /a/], [/a/, /a/, /a/], [/a/, /a/, /a/].
The *[A]* on the bus goes [/a/, /a/, /a/]
As in *[apple]*!

Teresa Phillips
Belle Terre Elementary
Palm Coast, FL

Tempting Words

High-frequency words

To prepare, write on a class supply of cookie cutouts different high-frequency words. Also write the words on a list for your reference. Place the cookies in a plastic cookie jar. Invite each child, in turn, to take a cookie from the jar and silently read the word. Then chant the question shown, inserting one of the words from the list. The child with the matching word replies as shown and then returns his cookie to the jar. Play continues until all the cookies are back in the jar.

Teacher: Who took the *[go]* cookie from the cookie jar?
Student: I took the *[go]* cookie from the cookie jar!

Erin Hammond
Leavenworth Elementary
Leavenworth, IN

Toss It!

To prepare for this small-group game, glue a copy of each card from page 152 to a separate paper plate. Arrange the plates on the floor in an open area. Invite a student to toss a beanbag until it lands on a plate. Then have her remove the beanbag, name the picture, and say its beginning (or ending) letter. If she is correct, she picks up the plate and sets it aside. If she is incorrect, have the other group members help her but leave the plate in place. Play continues until all the plates have been removed.

Katie Zuehlke
Bendix Elementary
Annandale, MN

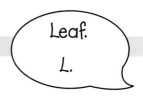

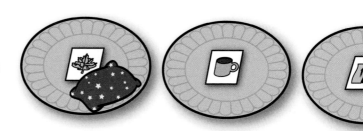

A Tall Book

These student-made booklets are just right for your kindergartners. To make a booklet, cut a sheet of copy paper in half to make two 5½" x 8½" pieces. Stack the pieces and fold them in half lengthwise to make a four-page booklet. Staple the booklet to the top of a 2" x 11" strip, as shown, to make a *T*. Give each child a *T* booklet. Have him write the sentence shown on the cover. On each remaining page, encourage him to complete the sentence "A _____ is tall" and add an illustration. Invite youngsters to read and reread their booklets to practice their reading skills.

Seema R. Gersten
Hillel Hebrew Academy
Beverly Hills, CA

Stretch and Say

Here's a visual way to help students sound out words. To prepare, accordion-fold a long strip of construction paper. Then, on separate blank cards, write different CVC words. Cut each word apart between the onset and the rime. Next, paper-clip the onset of a word to the left side of the strip and the rime to the right side.

Show students the strip with the cards stretched apart. Have them say the sound of the onset and the rime. Then lead them in blending the sounds as you slowly bring the cards together. Next, repeat the activity to segment the word by pulling the cards apart as youngsters say the sounds.

adapted from an idea by Tammy Fournier
Chaffee Elementary
Oxford, MA

Building Reading Skills

Bug Jug

Word family -ug

Students go buggy while reading and writing words in the *-ug* word family! To prepare, write different *-ug* words on copies of the bug cards on page 153. Invite each child to decorate the front of a small clasp envelope to look like a jar or jug. Then have her label it like the one shown. Next, direct each youngster to read the word on each bug and then put it in her jug. Encourage students to take home their envelopes for more practice.

Sarah Lindh
Riverview School
Silver Lake, WI

See page 157 for an activity that reinforces the **-et** word family.

Word Nests

High-frequency words

Make reading words "eggs-traordinary!" For each child, write different high-frequency words on several egg cutouts. Have each child cut out a copy of the bird pattern on page 153. After she glues the cutout to the front of a paper lunch bag, invite her to place her eggs in the bag. To practice reading the words, direct each youngster to remove one egg at a time. Have her place the words she can read in one pile and the words she needs help reading in another. Then help each student read the words in her help pile. Once a student can read all her words, give her a new batch of eggs for more practice.

Jody Steed
La Vega Primary Center
Waco, TX

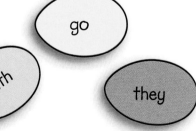

What's the Buzz?

Reading comprehension

Students retell a story with the help of a bumblebee! After a student hears a story or reads a book, give him a copy of page 154. Encourage him to write or draw to complete the graphic organizer. Next, have him cut out the bee pattern. Then help him tape one end of a length of string to the bee and the other end to the back of his paper. Invite each youngster to move the bee to each section of the hive as he tells the story to a partner.

Ana Catasus
Mother of Christ Catholic School
Miami, FL

Name Cooper — Reading comprehension

Title
The Very Hungry Caterpillar

Beginning
It came out of an egg.

Middle
It ate a lot of food.

End
It turned into a butterfly.

Toss and Tell

Letter-sound correspondence

To prepare for this small-group game, program sheets of construction paper with different letters. Spread out the papers on the floor. Invite each child, in turn, to toss a beanbag onto a paper. Then have him name the letter, its sound, and a word that begins with that letter. If desired, write each response on a sheet of chart paper labeled with the letter. Then display the lists for students to use as references.

Christine Huckins
Kindercare Learning Center
Fayetteville, NC

R.
/r/.
Rabbit.

A Sweet Story

High-frequency word booklet

Use this engaging booklet to reinforce one-to-one correspondence, high-frequency words, rhyming, or punctuation. Give each child a copy of pages 155 and 156. Then lead students in following the directions below to complete a booklet.

Ada Goren
Winston-Salem, NC

Directions for each child:
1. Booklet page 1: Color the lollipops to match the text.
2. Booklet pages 2 and 3: Color the pictures.
3. Booklet page 4: Color the lollipop red or blue to show which one you would rather have.
4. Cut out the pages and put them in order. Then staple the pages at the top between two construction paper covers.
5. Glue a large craft stick to the back cover.

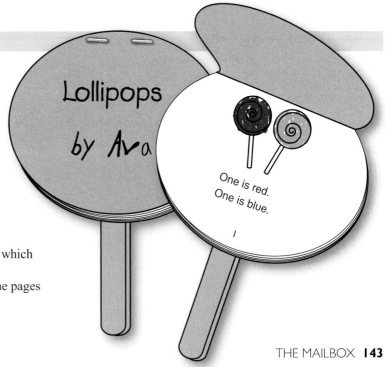

Lollipops
by Ava

One is red.
One is blue.
1

Building Reading Skills

Zoom! Zoom!

Phonological awareness

These small-group activities provide plenty of hands-on practice! Give each child three toy cars. Then choose an option below.

Blending words: Name a word that has three sounds, saying each sound in isolation. As each child blends the sounds to say the word, he positions the cars together, moving one car per sound.

Segmenting words: Have each child position his cars side by side so they are touching. Name a word that has three sounds. As each student slowly repeats the word, he moves one car per sound.

Angie Kelley
Weaver Elementary
Weaver, AL

See page 160 for a **skill sheet** that reinforces following written directions.

Map.

/m/, /a/, /p/.

Friend or Foe?

Main characters

Students make text-to-self connections with this story-related idea. Help each youngster identify a main character in a story of his choice. Have him use craft supplies to make his version of the character. Then invite each youngster, in turn, to share his craft and tell why the character would or would not be a good friend.

Erin Owens
Mupu School
Santa Paula, CA

Eggbert would be a good friend because he would care about my feelings.

How Many Are Home?

Word families

To prepare for this word-writing activity, label a simple house cutout with a different rime for each small group. To play, group members take turns writing on the house words that include the rime. After a predetermined amount of time, play stops and students count to see how many occupants (words) are in each house. **For an easier version,** write the words on each group's house. For each child's turn, she reads one of the words.

Amy Kallelis, Cold Spring Elementary, Doylestown, PA

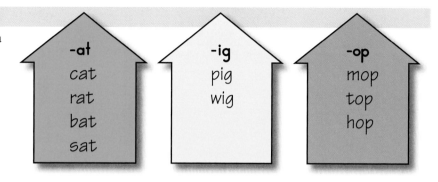

-at
cat
rat
bat
sat

-ig
pig
wig

-op
mop
top
hop

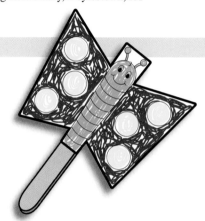

High-Flying Fun

Reading environmental print

Have each child color and cut out a copy of the butterfly pattern on page 159. Next, help her tape her butterfly to a craft stick to make a pointer. Then encourage her to "flutter" around the room in search of words. For each word she finds, she uses her pointer to track from left to right as she reads the word.

Ada Goren
Winston-Salem, NC

Word Wall Baseball

High-frequency words

For this baseball-themed game, write different high-frequency words on individual baseball cutouts (patterns on page 159). To set up the game, draw a baseball diamond on the board and place four magnets (players) near home plate. Then select a student to be your helper (catcher).

To play, lead youngsters in singing the song shown. During Line 3 of the song, give a student a baseball cutout. If he reads the word correctly at the end of the song, he moves a player to first base. If he reads the word incorrectly, he asks the catcher for help before trying again. As students continue to read words correctly, have them move the players around the bases as in the traditional game of baseball.

adapted from an idea by Heather Gustafson
José de Diego Community Academy
Chicago, IL

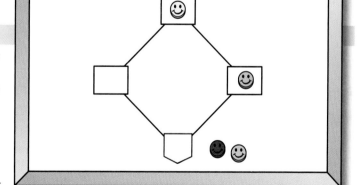

said

(sung to the tune of "Take Me Out to the Ballgame")

This is a special ball game.
Read a word; get a hit!
Here comes the pitch; this word's just for you.
If you need help, oh, you know what to do!
You can ask for clues from the catcher,
And then you try once again!
For it's one, two, three,
Read the word!
Here we go again!

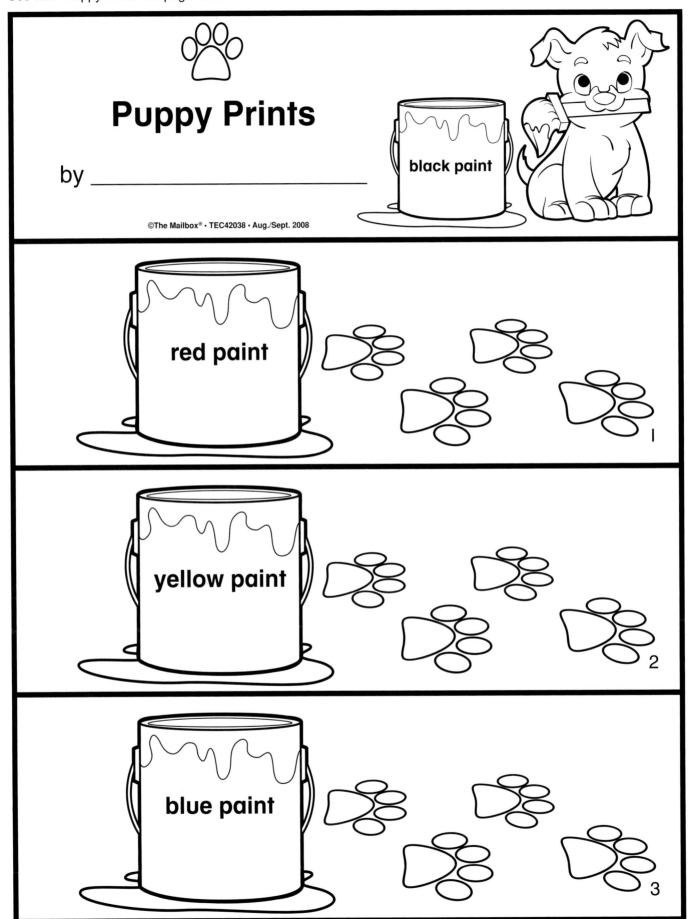

Puppy Prints

by _____

black paint

©The Mailbox® • TEC42038 • Aug./Sept. 2008

red paint

1

yellow paint

2

blue paint

3

©The Mailbox® • TEC42038 • Aug./Sept. 2008

My Book Report

book title

Here is a picture of the story.

Picture Cards

Use with "Toss It!" on page 141.

TEC42041 TEC42041 TEC42041 TEC42041

TEC42041 TEC42041 TEC42041 TEC42041

TEC42041 TEC42041 TEC42041 TEC42041

TEC42041 TEC42041 TEC42041 TEC42041

Bug Cards

Use with "Bug Jug" on page 142.

TEC42042
TEC42042
TEC42042
TEC42042
TEC42042
TEC42042

Bird Pattern

Use with "Word Nests" on page 142.

TEC42042

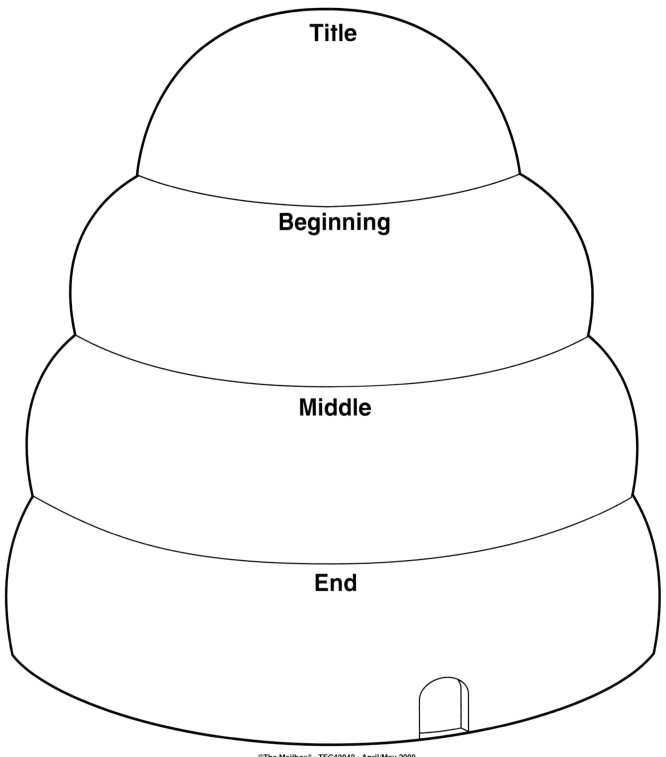

Title

Beginning

Middle

End

©The Mailbox® • TEC42042 • April/May 2009

Note to the teacher: Use with "What's the Buzz?" on page 143.

One is red.
One is blue.

1

Mom says, "One."
I say, "Two."

2

"One," Mom says.
And so I pick.

3

Which one would
you pick to lick?

4

Word Family Make-and-Read Activity: -et words

Have each child cut out a copy of the cards and word list below. Instruct her to form words with the cards, read the words, and then write them on a sheet of paper. Invite her to take the cards and word list home in an envelope for practice. If desired, follow up with the activity on page 158.

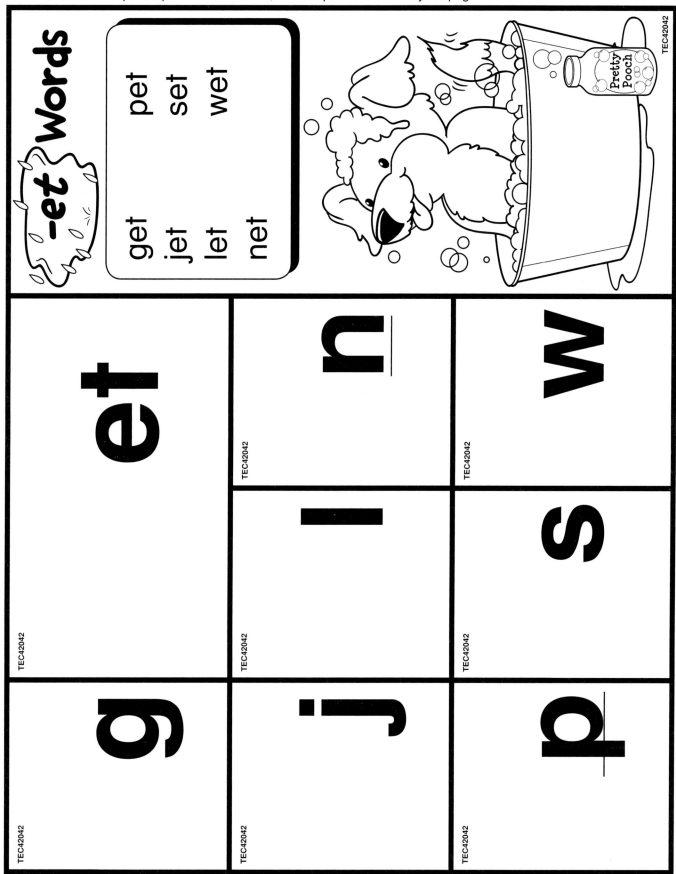

-et Words

get	pet
jet	set
let	wet
net	

et

n

w

i

s

g

j

p

A Wet Pet

 Cut.

Glue.

1. I [____] a tub.

2. My [____] is set.

3. I [____] him out.

4. I get all [____]!

©The Mailbox® • TEC42042 • April/May 2009

| wet | get | pet | let |

Note to the teacher: If desired, use with the word family make-and-read activity on page 157.

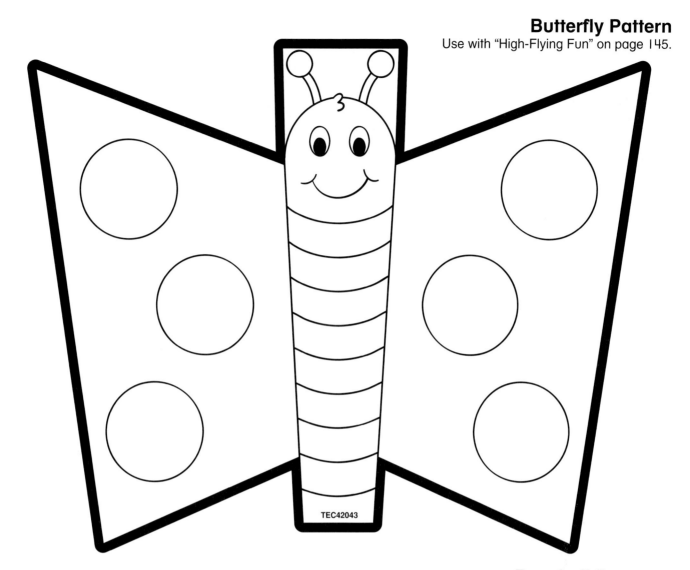

Butterfly Pattern
Use with "High-Flying Fun" on page 145.

TEC42043

Baseball Patterns
Use with "Word Wall Baseball" on page 145.

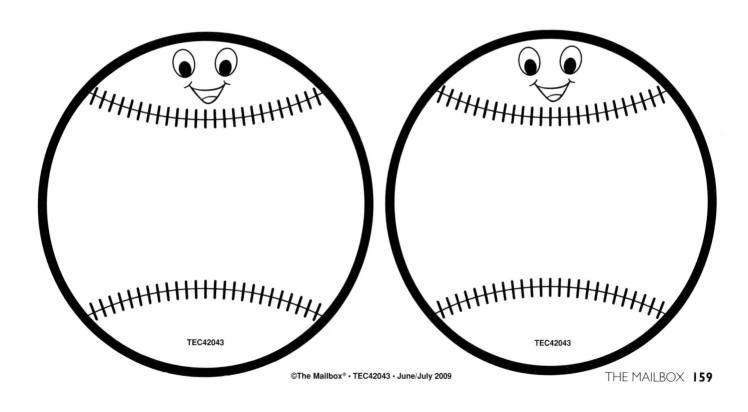

TEC42043

TEC42043

Name _____

Sunny Day

Read and do.

1. Color the ☀ yellow.
   sun

2. Color the ∿∿∿ green.
   grass

3. Color the 🦋 orange.
   butterfly

4. Color the 🪵 brown.
   log

5. Color the 🐦 blue.
   bird

6. Color **2** 🌼 purple.
   two flowers

7. Color **3** 🌼 red.
   three flowers

8. Draw and color a 🐝 .
   bee

Each child cuts out a copy of the cards below and sorts them on a copy of page 162. For additional practice, he puts the cards in a resealable plastic bag; then he takes the cards and mat home. For assessment, he completes a copy of the activity below.

Name _____

Phonological Awareness
Hearing middle sounds

Go to the Beach!

Color the pictures with ă as in .

Like Crab?

Sorting Mat

ă as in

Note to the teacher: Use with the sorting activity on page 161.

'TIS THE SEASON

'Tis the Season

Story and Safety

Back-to-school means back to buses! Arrange for a bus driver to have your students sit with her on a bus as she reads aloud a picture book version of "The Wheels on the Bus." Have her encourage the students to join in during a second reading. Then ask the driver to review bus rules and discuss what students should do if they just miss the bus, drop papers near the bus, or have other bus-related concerns.

Sandra O'Connell, Margaret M. Pierce Elementary, Remington, VA

Brief Introductions

These booklets help you get acquainted with students. Plus, they are great projects to share during open house! Help each child complete a paper with sentence starters like the ones shown. Then have him cut the sentences apart, glue each sentence on a separate sheet of paper, and add illustrations. Bind the papers between two covers and title the resulting book "A Snapshot of Me." Then mount a camera cutout to the front cover and a photo of the child to the inside of the book.

Andrea Patnaude
Anna McCabe Elementary
Smithfield, RI

> My name is **Carlos.**
>
> My favorite color is **blue.**
>
> When I am at home, I like to **ride my bike.**

Fall Domino Fun

For this small-group game, choose an option below and make game cards as described. To begin a round, one player deals three cards to each player. She stacks the remaining cards facedown and sets the top card faceup on the playing surface. To take a turn, a player places a card beside a card in play so the adjacent domino sections match. For example, she may match the type of objects, the numbers, a number and a set of objects, or a number and a number word. If she does not have a matching card, she takes the top card from the stack. If she does not get a matching card, the next player takes a turn. Players take turns until they cannot play any more cards and no cards are left in the stack.

J. J. Markle, Hanover, PA

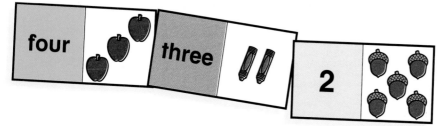

Numbers: Color and cut out two copies of the cards from page 170.
Number words: Color and cut out two copies of the cards from page 171.
Numbers and number words: Color and cut out one copy each of the cards from pages 170 and 171.

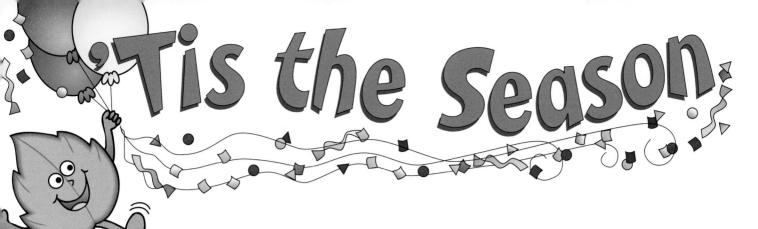

'Tis the Season

Tuneful Pumpkin

Display the song shown. After you teach it to students, program blank cards with chosen high-frequency words and ask youngsters to find the matching words in the song. Or instruct each youngster to draw a pumpkin like the one described. Then have him glue a copy of the song on his paper and point to the words as he reads them.

Faith Shiver, Camilla, GA

(sung to the tune of "I'm a Little Teapot")

*I'm an orange pumpkin, big and round.
Here is my vine that trails on the ground.
If you come and pick me, I will say,
"Please decorate me for Halloween day!"*

Chain of Thanks

For this Thanksgiving project, make a class supply of fall-colored paper strips. Ask each child to name something for which she is grateful; then write the information on an individual strip and have her write her name on the back of it. Instruct students to make a chain with the programmed strips. Display the completed chain as desired.

Rebekah Elder, University United Methodist Child Development Center, Fort Worth, TX

Find the Feathers!

To prepare this small-group game, cut out a copy of the spinner pattern on page 173. Then attach a paper clip to it with a brad. For each player, glue a turkey head to a small paper plate and make one feather of each of the eight basic colors. (See the patterns on page 172.) Put the feathers in the center of the group.

To take a turn, a player spins the spinner and reads the word on which it lands. If his turkey does not have a feather of the corresponding color, he tucks the end of a matching feather under his plate. If his turkey already has a matching feather, he does nothing. The players take turns as described for the allotted time or until one player's turkey has eight feathers. Then the players compare how many feathers their turkeys have. **For an easier version,** color each section of the spinner the corresponding color.

Andrea Singleton, Waynesville Elementary, Waynesville, OH

'Tis the Season

Catching Snowflakes

To prepare for this small-group game, draw on the board three circles (snowballs) and label each with a different ending letter: -d, -p, or -t. Place in a bag one snowflake card (page 173) per child. Say to students, "It is 'snowing' ending sounds," as you pour the cards out of the bag. In turn, have each youngster pick up a card, say the pictured word's ending sound and letter, and then line up by the corresponding snowball.

adapted from an idea by Kristin Bauer Ganoung, Halsey, NE

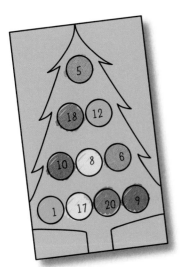

Trim the Tree

Put a seasonal twist on number recognition with this class game! Write the numbers from 1 to 20 on the board. Give each child a copy of the tree card on page 173 and have her copy a different posted number in each ornament. To play, announce a number from the board. Each child who has the matching number on her card lightly colors the corresponding ornament. (Be sure to keep track of each number called.) When a student has colored all her ornaments, she announces, "My tree is trimmed!" **For a phonics version,** have students program the ornaments with letters. Then announce words and have students identify the beginning letter.

Staci Peterson, Voyager Elementary, Alexandria, MN

Little Snowman

Teach students the song shown. Then have each youngster fold a sheet of paper in half and unfold it. On one half, instruct her to draw a picture of the snowman from the song before it melted. On the other half, have her draw a picture of the snowman after it melted. Post the pictures along with a copy of the song for all to see!

Abby Clark, Sandoval Grade School, Sandoval, IL

(sung to the tune of "I'm a Little Teapot")

I'm a little snowman,
Short and fat.
I've a carrot nose
And a black top hat.
When it gets much warmer,
Look at me.
Watch me melt.
Now what do you see?

See page 174 for a **skill sheet** that reinforces syllables.

Groundhog Homes

To prepare for this initial-consonant activity, give each student a foam cup and a groundhog cutout (pattern on page 175) attached to a craft stick. Have her decorate the cup to make a burrow for the groundhog. Then help her push the end of the stick through the bottom of the cup so the groundhog can easily move up and down. Write a letter on the board and then name a word. If the word begins with the letter, instruct students to push the groundhog from its burrow. If the word does not begin with the letter, the groundhog remains in its burrow.

adapted from an idea by Andrea Singleton, Waynesville Elementary
Waynesville, OH

A Presidential Tune

Display a map of the United States and point out the location of Washington, DC. After sharing with students that the president lives in Washington, DC, lead them in singing the song below.

(sung to the tune of "The Muffin Man")

Oh, do you know the president,
The president, the president?
Oh, do you know the president
Who lives in Washington, DC?

Oh, yes, we know the president,
The president, the president.
Oh, yes, we know the president;
His name is [president's name].

Coramarie Marinan, Howe Elementary, Green Bay, WI

Looking for Gold

For this whole-group activity, label a class supply of pot-shaped cutouts with different numbers. Arrange the pots on the floor to form a large circle. Have all but one student (the leprechaun) join you in sitting behind a pot. Invite the leprechaun to stand in the middle of the circle and cover her eyes while you secretly hide a coin cutout under a pot. Ask the leprechaun to uncover her eyes and name the number on the pot she thinks the coin is under. If she does not find the coin in three guesses, give her clues to help her identify the correct number. Once the pot is identified, have the leprechaun and the student sitting behind the coin switch places to play again.

Taimi Kelley, Dennis Township Primary School
Cape May Court House, NJ

See page 176 for a **skill sheet** that reinforces patterning.

'Tis the Season

Scrambled Sums

For this addition activity, give each child a large plastic egg and a supply of counters. Have each youngster open her egg. Then, as you announce an addition story problem, direct each student to place counters in each egg half to match the problem. Next, ask her to close her egg and shake it up. To find the sum, have each youngster "crack" open her egg and count the counters. After she writes the corresponding number sentence on a sheet of paper, announce a different story problem for another round.

Mary Ruth Downs, Community Christian School
Metcalfe, Ontario, Canada

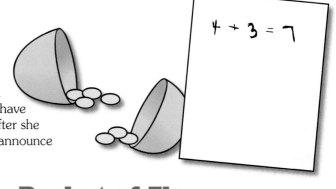

Basket of Flowers

These beautiful blossoms give youngsters word family practice. On a copy of page 177, write a different rime on the center of each flower; then copy the page to make a class supply. A child writes on the petals of each flower different words using the flower's rime. After each petal has a word, he cuts out the flowers and tapes a pipe cleaner (stem) to the back of each.

To make a flower basket, each student paints the outside of an individual-size milk carton (with the top cut off). When the paint is dry, he places a small ball of clay inside the carton and inserts the flower stems in the clay. Complete the basket by stapling a construction paper handle to the top of the carton.

Barbara Rice, North Street School, Windsor Locks, CT

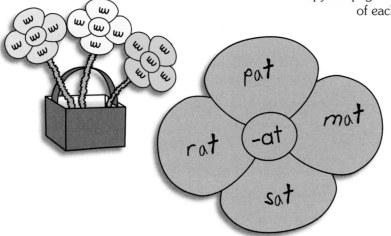

Buzzing Along

Program a class supply of yellow hexagon cutouts (honeycomb cells) to match one of the options below. Attach the honeycomb cells to the floor to make a path. Then invite your busy bees to join you for some learning fun.

Letter-sound correspondence: Label the honeycomb cells with letters. Invite students to make a buzzing sound as they slowly move along the path. When you say, "Stop!" each youngster stops on a cell. Then have each child, in turn, announce the letter and its sound.

Number recognition: Label the honeycomb cells with numbers. Have youngsters make a quiet buzzing sound as they move along the path. When you call out a number, the student(s) who is on or closest to the number you called makes a loud buzzing sound.

High-frequency words: Label the honeycomb cells with words. Have youngsters quietly read each word as they walk along the path. After a short amount of time, announce one of the words. Each child standing on a cell with that word makes a buzzing sound as he travels to the hive (a predetermined area of the room).

adapted from an idea by Roberta M. Neff, Espy Elementary, Kenton, OH

'Tis the Season

At the Beach

To encourage creative writing, place writing paper at a center along with a tote bag containing beach-related items. A youngster looks in the bag and names each item. She refers to items to jumpstart her thinking about a beach story. Then she writes and illustrates a story about a day at the beach.

adapted from an idea by Ada Goren
Winston-Salem, NC

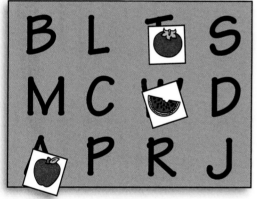

A Perfect Picnic

Serve up some practice with letters and sounds with this small-group activity. To prepare, cut apart a tagboard copy of the cards on page 179 and place them in a picnic basket. Then program a plastic tablecloth with the beginning letters of the foods on the cards. In turn, each child takes a card from the basket, names the pictured food, and places it on the tablecloth atop the corresponding beginning letter. **For an added challenge,** write a few extra letters on the tablecloth as distracters.

Sheli Gosset
Woodlawn Elementary
Sebring, FL

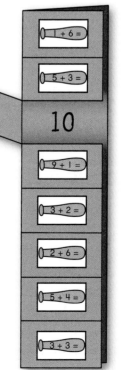

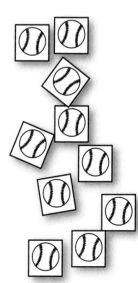

Home-Run Addition

To begin, help each child fold a 12" x 18" sheet of construction paper in half and then cut the top flap into eight sections as shown. Each youngster cuts out the baseball counters and bat cards from a copy of page 180. Then she glues a bat card to the front of each flap. Next, she uses the ball counters as manipulatives to solve the problem on a card. After writing the sum under the matching flap, she continues to solve the remaining problems.

Jennifer Marshall
Naples, FL

See page 178 for a **skill sheet**.

Domino Cards

Use with "Fall Domino Fun" on page 164.

(4 crayons) TEC42038	**1**	(5 acorns) TEC42038	(3 apples)
(5 pencils) TEC42038	**2**	**5**	**5** TEC42038
(2 apples) TEC42038	**3**	**3** TEC42038	(1 crayon)
(3 acorns) TEC42038	**4**	**2**	(5 acorns) TEC42038
(1 bus) TEC42038	**5**	**1** TEC42038	(2 buses)

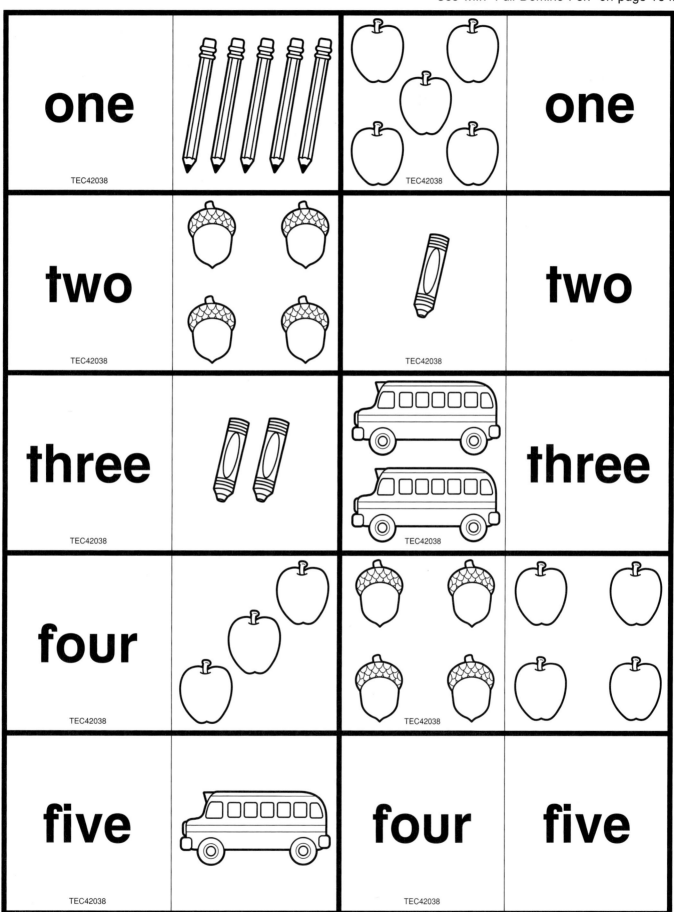

one			one
two			two
three			three
four			
five		four	five

TEC42038

Spinner, Turkey, and Feather Patterns
Use with "Find the Feathers!" on page 165.

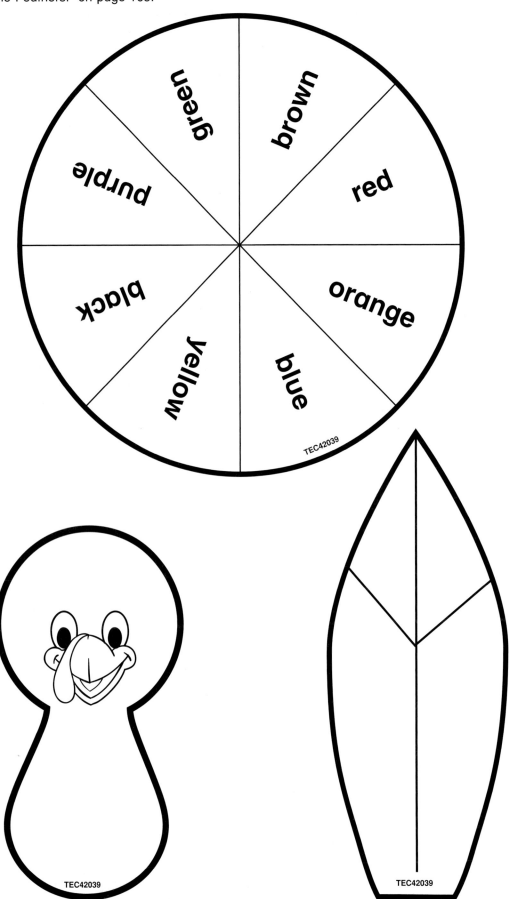

green
brown
purple
red
black
orange
yellow
blue

TEC42039

TEC42039

TEC42039

Snowflake Cards

Use with "Catching Snowflakes" on page 166.

Tree Card

Use with "Trim the Tree" on page 166.

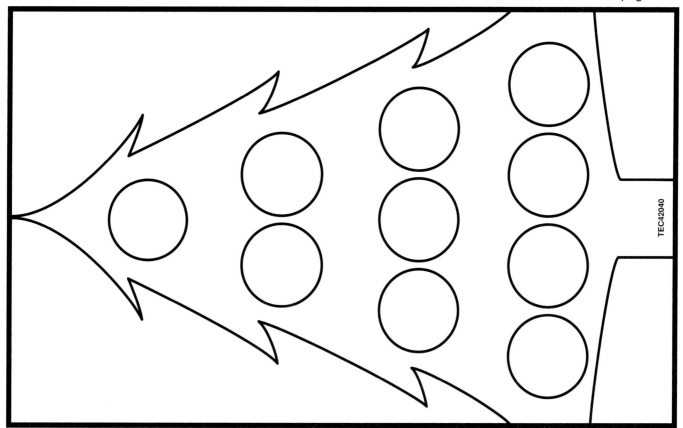

Keeping Warm

Name each picture.

Count the word parts.

Color a mitten for each word part.

©The Mailbox® • TEC42040 • Dec./Jan. 2008–9

Groundhog Patterns

Use with "Substitute Groundhog" on page 24 and "Groundhog Homes" on page 167.

Name

Coins, Coins, Coins!

Cut.

Glue to finish the patterns.

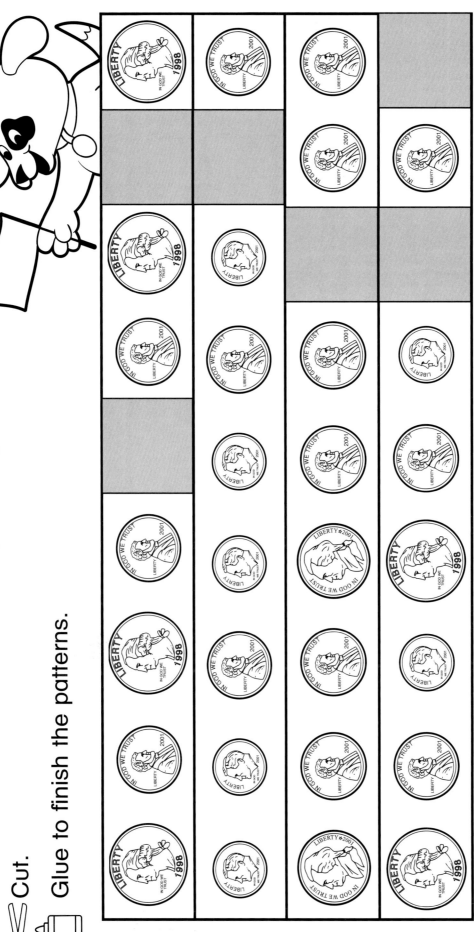

A.

B.

C.

D.

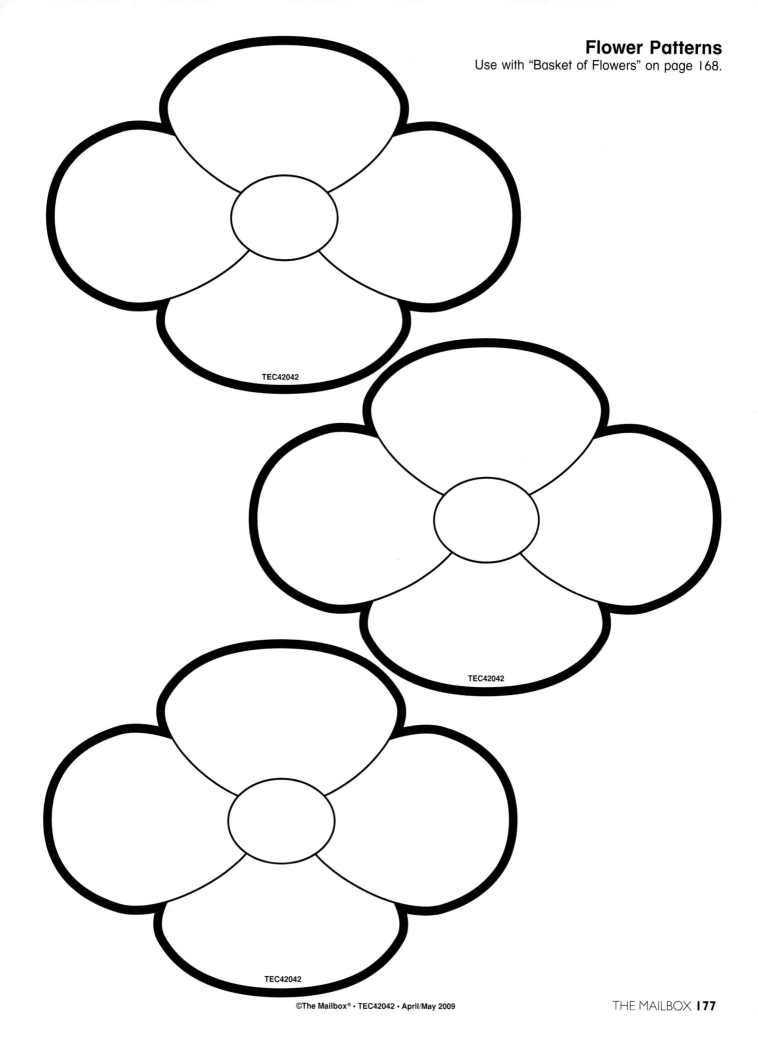

TEC42042

TEC42042

TEC42042

Name _____

In the Garden

✂ Cut. 🧴 Glue to make a graph.

How Many Vegetables?

🥕 carrots					
🌰 radishes					
🥬 lettuce					

✏ Write how many.

🥕 _____

🌰 _____

🥬 _____

✏ Circle.

Which has **more?**

Which has **fewer?**

Which has the **most?**

©The Mailbox® • TEC42042 • April/May 2009

TEC42043

TEC42043

TEC42043

JUICE

TEC42043

TEC42043

TEC42043

TEC42043

TEC42043

TEC42043

TEC42043

MILK

TEC42043

RAISINS

TEC42043

Baseball Counters and Bat Cards
Use with "Home-Run Addition" on page 169.

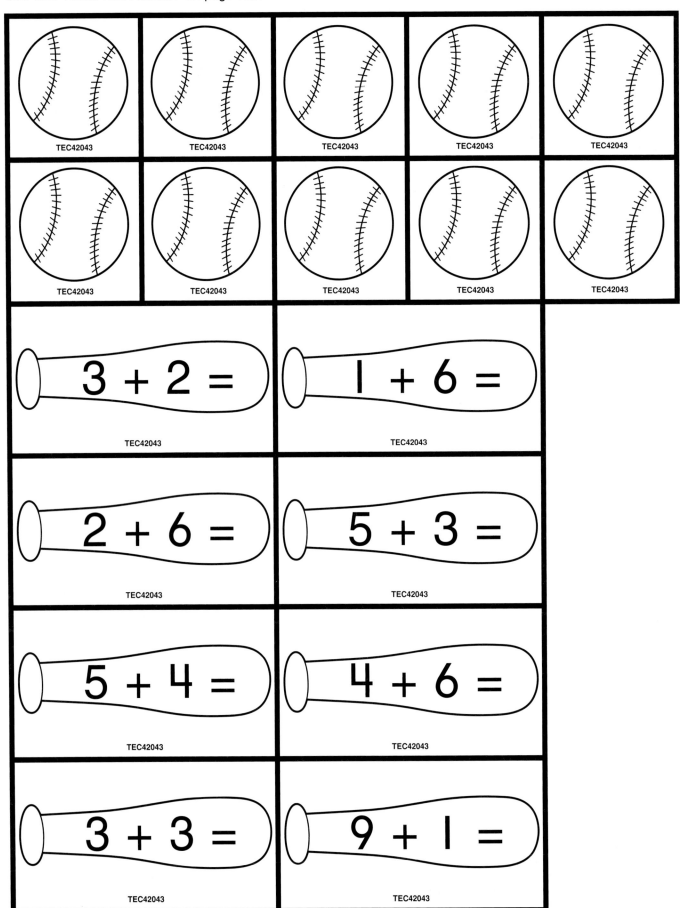

3 + 2 =

TEC42043

1 + 6 =

TEC42043

2 + 6 =

TEC42043

5 + 3 =

TEC42043

5 + 4 =

TEC42043

4 + 6 =

TEC42043

3 + 3 =

TEC42043

9 + 1 =

TEC42043

For Me?

Lotto game (initial consonants or high-frequency words): To make caller's cards, cut out a copy of one set of cards from page 182. (To call a space for the initial consonant game, name the corresponding consonant.) Give each child a copy of this page and a copy of the appropriate game cards. Ask him to cut out the cards and glue each card to a randomly chosen board space. Then give students game markers and have them play the game like traditional lotto.

Game Cards

Use with "For Me?" on page 181.

Initial Consonant Picture Cards

High-Frequency Word Cards

and	can
he	it
me	like
see	to
you	my
go	not

Yum, Carrots!

Lotto game (time to the hour or -an and -at words): To make caller's cards, cut out a copy of one set of cards from page 184. Give each child a copy of this page and a copy of the appropriate game cards. Ask him to cut out the cards and glue each card to a randomly chosen board space. Then give students game markers and have them play the game like traditional lotto.

Game Cards

Use with the lotto game on page 183.

Clock Cards

-an and *-at* Word Cards

an	at
fan	bat
man	cat
ran	hat
tan	pat
van	sat

Tip: Give students orange squares (carrots) to use as game markers. Encourage them to listen carefully to the times or words you call so they can fill their baskets with carrots.

Name

What a Melon!

©The Mailbox® · TEC42043 · June/July 2009

Game Cards

Use with "What a Melon!" on page 185.

Subtraction Cards

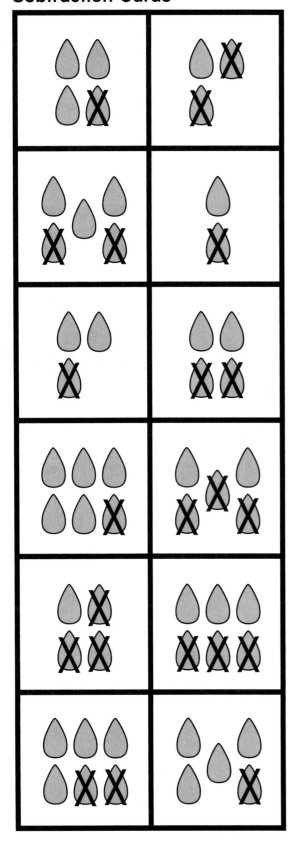

Word Cards

den	let
hen	met
men	pet
pen	set
ten	vet
get	wet

WHAT WORKS FOR YOU?

What Works for You?

Lesson Planning

I write my daily schedule across a long, narrow strip that I cut from a colorful file folder. I laminate the strip and then clip it to the top of the current week's pages in my plan book. It saves me time since I don't need to write the schedule each week! *Vicki Braddy, Southern Boone County Primary School, Ashland, MO*

A color-coded plan book works well for me! I copy my schedule on five different colors of paper—one for each day of the week—and then secure the pages in a three-ring binder. The color coding helps me remember details unique to certain days of the week, and the format gives me extra writing space. *Brenda Wilson, Macon Elementary, Macon, MO*

Since plans can change at a moment's notice in kindergarten, I write my plans on sticky notes and then attach them to my plan book. I can rearrange the notes as needed while keeping my plan book neat. *Dawn King, Harwich Elementary, Harwich, MA*

To help me remember specific ideas from *The Mailbox*® magazine, I label page dividers with different skill areas and put them in a three-ring binder. I keep notes about ideas and copies of activities in the appropriate sections of the binder. *Amy Spence, Harvest Baptist Christian School, Medford, OR*

I put poems and songs on large index cards and file them by theme. When it's time to plan a thematic unit, I simply flip through the cards to see what I have on the topic. *Beth Harkcom, William H. Blount Elementary, Wilmington, NC*

What Works for YOU?

Journal Time

I have a few tricks up my sleeve to help inspire my kindergartners during journal writing time! On days when ideas are running low, I provide an assortment of magazine pictures. Each student chooses one to glue in her journal and then writes about the picture. The idea also works with stickers or stencils to trace. *Tammy Riché, Maurice Elementary, Maurice, LA*

At the beginning of each month, I display an oversize cutout of a seasonal shape, such as a heart or shamrock. Then I lead the class in brainstorming words associated with the month, the season, or the month's holidays. Students refer to the word list throughout the month as they write in their journals. *Robin Winkler, Riverside Elementary, Fond du Lac, WI*

I use one-inch binders with clear pockets on the covers to hold my students' journal writing. At the start of each month, I provide a seasonal sheet for each youngster to color and put in the cover pocket. Daily writing is done on individual pages stored in the binder. At the end of the month, I take out the entries, staple them behind the monthly cover, and send the completed journal home. *Kelli Liles, Red Bank Elementary, Lexington, SC*

One day during the week, I invite my students to choose their journal topic. I write three words or phrases on the board, each beginning with our letter of the week, and read them aloud. Each child writes his name under his chosen topic and then writes about the topic in his journal. My class loves Pick a Topic Day! *Heather Keller, Valley Brook School, Long Valley, NJ*

I cut 70-page spiral notebooks in half to use as journals in my classroom. I can make two kindergarten-size journals from one notebook! *Kelly Kramer, Rivercrest Elementary, Bartlett, TN*

What Works for You?

Managing Art Projects

To help youngsters keep track of all the cutout pieces of a craft project, I give each child a personalized clothespin. As a child cuts out a project piece, she clips it with her clothespin. That way important pieces aren't accidentally thrown away or mixed in with a classmate's cutouts. *Alexis Thaw-Kaufman, Riverside Elementary, Rockville Centre, NY*

I save empty spice and seasoning shakers to use in my art center. After cleaning them, I fill the shakers with glitter, sequins, or small beads. Youngsters can control the amount needed for a project, and I can control the mess! *Victoria-Ann Rogers, Missouri State University, Springfield, MO*

Kindergarteners often have difficulty adding a background— such as sky, clouds, and grass—to their easel paintings because the paint drips and runs down the rest of their pictures. To remedy this and add an interesting look to artwork, I have students omit the background. Once a picture's paint has dried, I invite the student to fill the white space with a crayon or chalk rubbing. *Diane Bonica, Deer Creek Elementary, Tigard, OR*

My students use small paintbrushes to apply glue to their art projects. The brushes help youngsters use just the right amount of glue, but cleaning them can be a sticky situation! Soaking the bristles in full-strength liquid fabric softener makes the glue rinse right off, and they smell nice too! *Judy Ober, Prettyboy HomeBase, Freeland, MD*

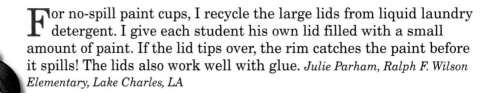

For no-spill paint cups, I recycle the large lids from liquid laundry detergent. I give each student his own lid filled with a small amount of paint. If the lid tips over, the rim catches the paint before it spills! The lids also work well with glue. *Julie Parham, Ralph F. Wilson Elementary, Lake Charles, LA*

What Works for You?

End of the School Year

One day toward the end of the year, I ask my students to help me clean washable classroom items. I give each student duo a large ice cream tub (with a handle) filled with soapy water, a wash rag, and a towel. We go outside and wash items such as pattern blocks, LEGO pieces, and plastic toys. This activity is a great help to me, and my students love sharing the responsibility. *Deborah Patrick, Park Forest Elementary, State College, PA*

As I sort through my classroom at the end of the year, I set beginning-of-the-year materials aside in my "First Week of School" tub. This saves time and prepares me for the first week of kindergarten. *Paula R. Trueax, McNary Heights Elementary, Umatilla, OR*

First Week of School

For homework during the last two weeks of school, I ask my students to create pictures with sentences describing their favorite kindergarten memories. After my students share their work, I use the projects as decorations for my end-of-the-year celebration. *Suzanne Ward, Caledonia Centennial Public School, Caledonia, Ontario, Canada*

Toward the end of the school year, I ask each student to write and illustrate his best piece of advice to share with an upcoming kindergartner. At the beginning of the next school year, I display the words of wisdom on a bulletin board. My new students are always excited to see that kindergartners can write! *Stacy Buchmoyer, St. Catherine Laboure School, Harrisburg, PA*

For a simple and easy way to thank our volunteers, I have students work in groups to decorate the letters and exclamation point in "Thank You!" written on 12" x 18" paper as shown. Then I take a picture of my students holding their signs in order, make copies of the picture, and attach the photos to cards signed by the kids. My volunteers love these special mementos! *Brynn Dawson, Klickitat Elementary, Klickitat, WA*

Weekly Plan

Monday	Tuesday	Wednesday	Thursday	Friday

Note to the teacher: Make copies of this page to help you with your lesson planning.

WRITING

Write On!

On the Way

Here's a **prompt** to which every child can respond! Invite students to tell what they observed on the way to school. Guide them to describe details, such as color, size, and location. Then give each child a copy of page 196. Instruct her to illustrate her response to the question, encouraging her to include details like the ones discussed. Have her complete the sentence and then color the rest of the paper as desired.

Nancy Strout, Greater Portland Christian School, South Portland, ME

Drawing Stories

To encourage students to include **details in their illustrations**, tell them that you want to write a story about a student. Then use one crayon to draw a simple illustration of a secretly chosen youngster. Invite students to guess who the youngster is. After they share several guesses, wonder aloud whether a more detailed illustration would help tell the story. Then draw a similar illustration, this time using crayons that match the colors of the youngster's clothing and adding significant details. Guide students to identify the youngster if they did not already do so and have them compare the two drawings. Afterward, instruct each child to picture in his mind a story he would like to share. Then ask him to draw a corresponding illustration and write about it.

Rebecka Spence, Greensboro, NC

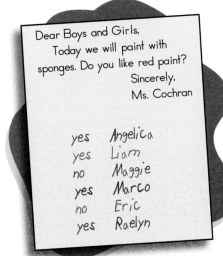

Variety at Group Time

Make the most of **morning messages**! Have students help you write a message each day as appropriate for their skills. Extend their learning with the options below.

Friday Find: Save the messages from the first four days of the week. Reread the messages on Friday and instruct students to draw different shapes around designated words.

Question Day: Include a yes-or-no question and ask students to write responses.

Puzzle Time: Cut the sentences apart. Have students cut the sentences between the words and then arrange the words in the correct order.

Marcia Cochran, Kalamazoo Christian West Preschool, Kalamazoo, MI

Write On!

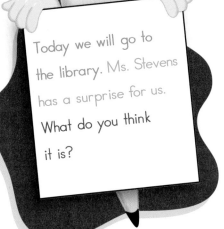

Today we will go to the library. Ms. Stevens has a surprise for us.

What do you think it is?

Colorful Clues

When you write a **morning message**, use a different-colored marker for each sentence. It's a simple way to help youngsters distinguish between words and sentences! For reinforcement, have students count the number of words in each sentence. Then ask youngsters to point out the beginning and end of each sentence and identify the corresponding uppercase letter and end mark.

Sara Miller, All Saints Episcopal School, Lubbock, TX

Over and Under

My Spider's Walk by Devin

My spider went over the table.

This "spider-rific" booklet is great for helping youngsters understand that their **illustrations and writing should match**. For each child, make one copy of page 197 and two copies of page 198. Cut out the cover and pages. Then staple the *over* and *under* pages between the cover and last page. To complete his booklet, have each youngster write his name on the cover. Instruct him to complete the sentence on each page and illustrate it. Then give him a length of string to which you have tied a plastic toy spider or spider ring. Ask him to tape the free end of the string to the web on the cover. When the child reads the booklet, have him use the spider to point to the words and act out the story.

Patsy James, Eisenhower Elementary, Boulder, CO

"Sense-ational" Apples

Apples
Round, yellow,
Crunchy, white,
Sweet, small,
Juicy, yummy, delicious,
Round, yellow.

Observation skills are the key to this **poetry idea**. Divide students into groups and place an apple in the center of each group. Then have students name words that describe how the apples look. List the words on the board. Next, cut the apples and give each child a slice. As the youngsters eat the apples, guide them to name different words that describe how the apples look. Also have them name words that tell how the apples sound, smell, feel, and taste. Add the words to the board. The next day, help each child write an apple poem similar to the one shown, using two or three describing words per line. Then have her mount the poem on an apple cutout.

Toni Walker, Southern Elementary, Lexington, KY

See pages 199-212 for **writing helpers.**

Name ______________________ Responding to a prompt

What Did You See?

Draw and write.

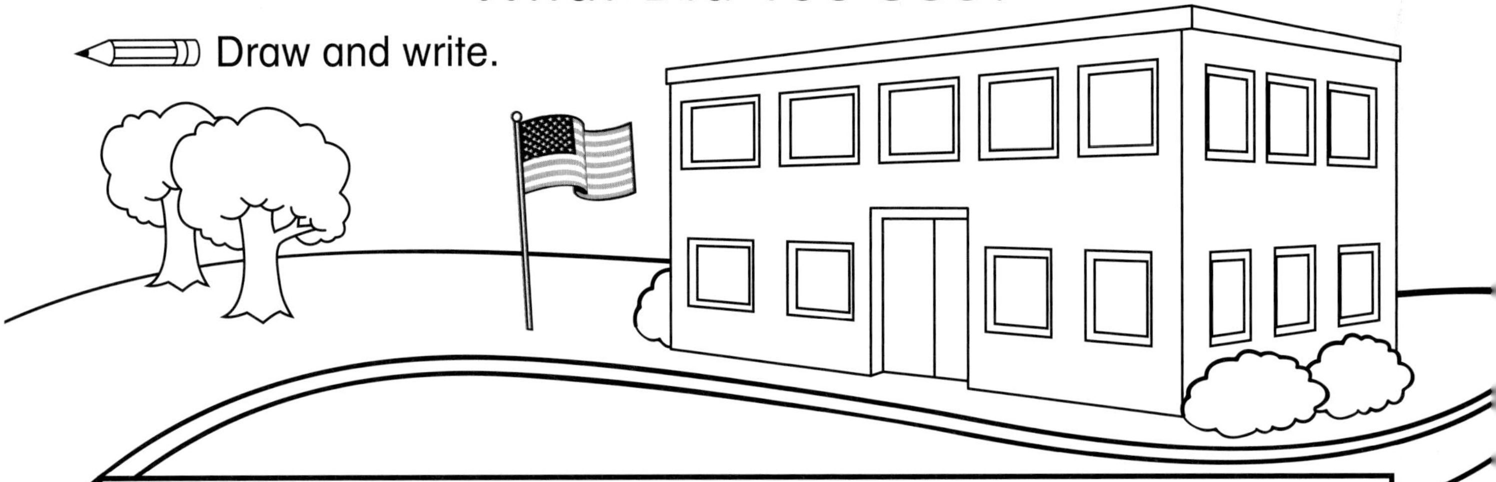

On the way to school, I saw ______________________

 Note to the teacher: Use with "On the Way" on page 194.

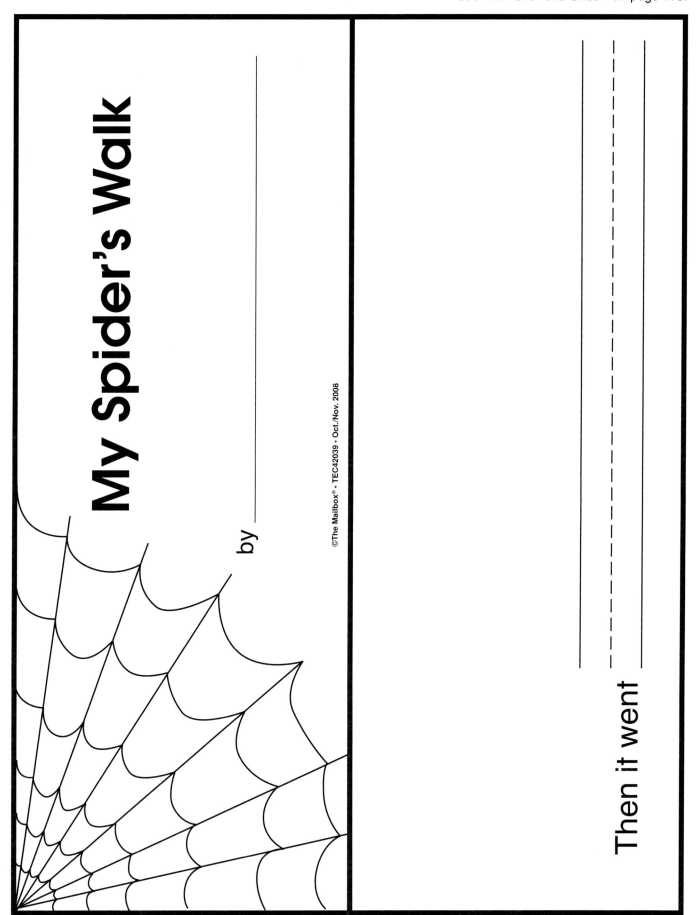

My Spider's Walk

by _____

©The Mailbox® • TEC42039 • Oct./Nov. 2008

Then it went _____

Booklet Pages

Use with "Over and Under" on page 195.

My spider went over the

My spider went under the

Winter Words

boots

scarf

hat

sled

mittens

snow

presents

snowman

Note to the teacher: Give each student a copy of this page. Have her write her name on it, color the illustrations, and then staple it in her journal.

Spring Words

 bee

 chick

 bird

 egg

 bug

 flower

 butterfly

 nest

Note to the teacher: Give each student a copy of this page. Have him write his name on it, color the illustrations, and then staple it in his journal.

Outdoor Words

 ball

 **skateboard**

 jump rope

 skip

 **kick**

 slide

 ride

 **swings**

 scooter

 **throw**

- -

Note to the teacher: Give each child a copy of this page. Ask her to keep the paper in her journal or writing folder for easy reference.

Color and cut apart a copy of the cards below. After you read and discuss each sentence starter with students, post it at a center for writing inspiration.

Snow is

When it is cold,

TEC42040

TEC42040

Color and cut apart a copy of the cards below. After you read and discuss each sentence starter with students, post the cards at a center for writing inspiration.

TEC42041

TEC42041

My friends

When it is windy,

Sentence Starter Cards

Color and cut apart a copy of the cards below. After you read and discuss
each sentence starter with students, post it at a center for writing inspiration.

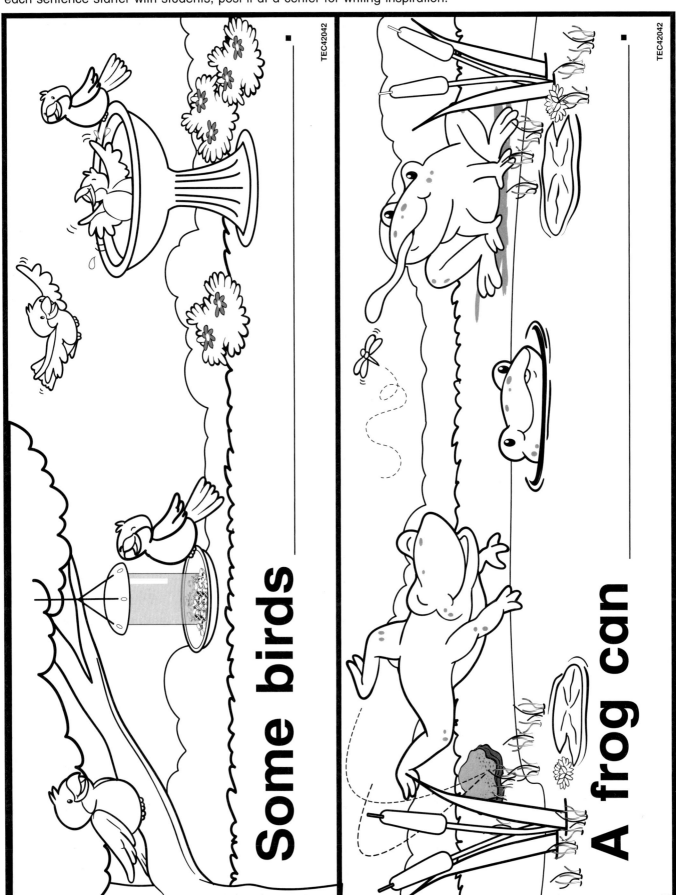

Some birds

A frog can

TEC42042

TEC42042

Color and cut apart a copy of the cards below. After you read and discuss each sentence starter with students, post the cards at a center for writing inspiration.

A picnic is

It is fun to

Graphic organizer

Winter Writing Ideas

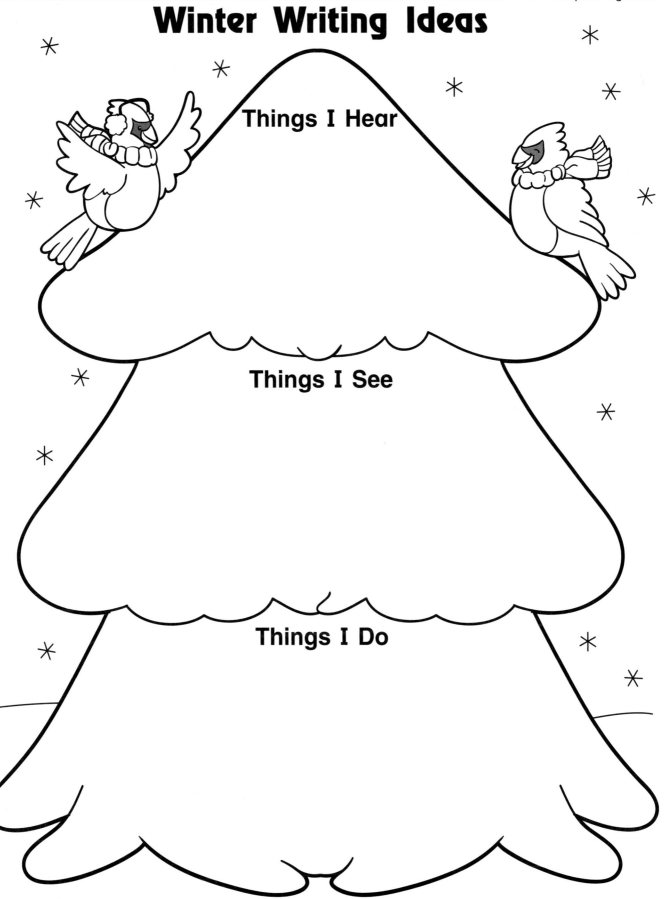

Things I Hear

Things I See

Things I Do

©The Mailbox® • TEC42040 • Dec./Jan. 2008–9

Note to the teacher: Give each child a copy of this page. Ask him to write or draw things he hears, sees, and does in the winter. Have him keep his completed paper in his journal or writing folder for easy reference.

Name _____

"Grrrreat" Writing Ideas

Draw 4 things you did yesterday.

Write.

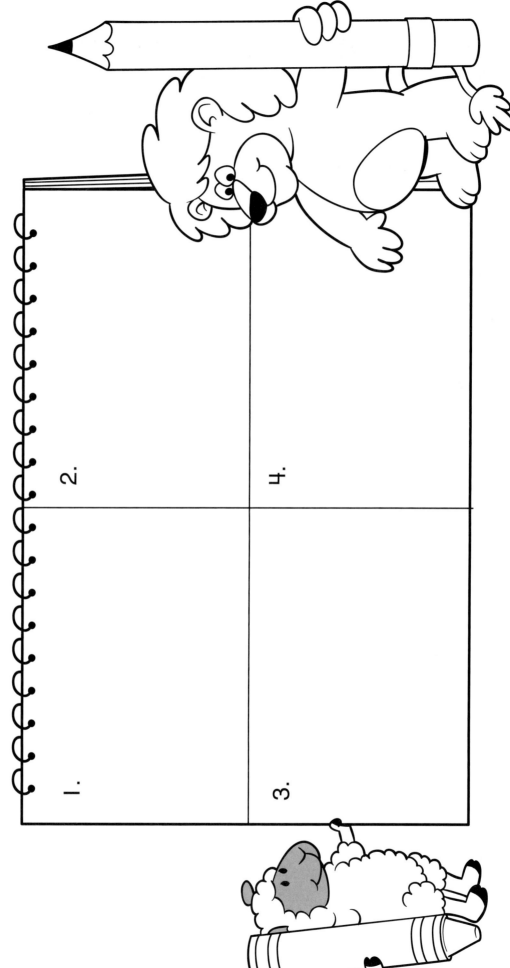

1.

2.

3.

4.

©The Mailbox® • TEC42041 • Feb./Mar. 2009

Note to the teacher: Give each child a copy of this page. Instruct him to draw in each box something he did yesterday and have him label each drawing. Ask him to keep the paper in his journal or writing folder. Encourage him to refer to the paper when he needs a writing idea.

Writing Helper

Summer Words

ice cream		beach
picnic		bee
sun		bike
swim		bug

☐ A hot day…

☐ The sun…

☐ Summer is…

☐ A bee…

☐ Bugs can…

☐ The beach is…

Note to the teacher: Have each child keep a copy of this page in his journal or writing folder. After he uses a prompt, ask him to draw a check mark in its box.

Sweet Dreams!

Think: What do you do when it is time for bed?

Draw. What I Do First   What I Do Next

Write.

Name _____

High-Flying Friends

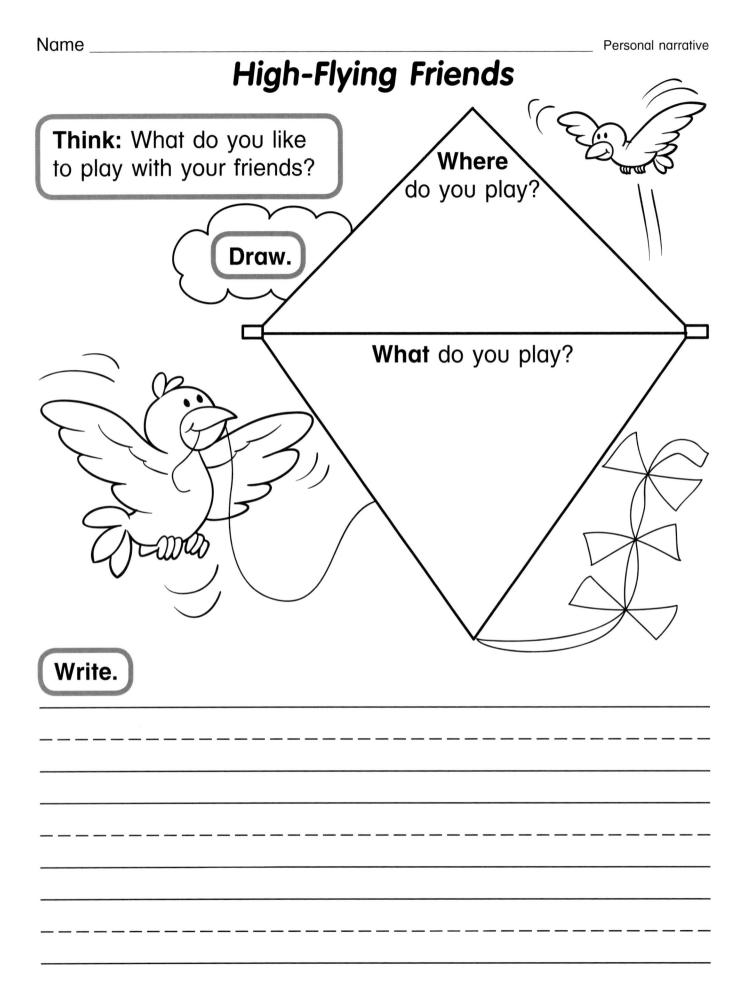

Think: What do you like to play with your friends?

Draw.

Where do you play?

What do you play?

Write.

_____
_ _
_____
_ _
_____
_ _
_____

Name _____

Pitter-patter!

Think: Think about a day it rained.

Draw.

Show two things you did.

Write.

_____

- -

_____

- -

_____

- -

_____

- -

_____

On the Go

Think: When have you gone someplace fun?

Draw.

Where did you go?

What did you do?

Write.

_____

_____

_____

_____

_____

_____

©The Mailbox® • TEC42043 • June/July 2009

LITERACY UNITS

Rhyming Fun for Everyone!

Ready Rhythm

Your students will be eager to do several rounds of this chant! Sit in a circle with students and establish a steady beat by alternately clapping and patting your lap. Encourage students to join in. Next, say the chant shown, pausing for students to echo each line. Then say a word, point to a chosen youngster, and have him say a rhyming word. Repeat the chant to begin another round.

We're going on a rhyming hunt.
I know what to do.
I need to listen well
And rhyme that word for you.

Heather E. Graley, Grace Christian School, Blacklick, OH

Race to the Place!

To prepare this partner center, color a copy of the gameboard on page 216. Label one side of a plastic math chip "1" and the other side "2." Then put the math chip in a disposable cup and set out two game markers. Have each player place her game marker on a different car. To take a turn, a player shakes the cup and spills out the math chip. Then she advances the corresponding number of spaces and follows any instructions where she lands. If she lands on a space with a picture, she names the picture and a rhyming word. (Encourage players not to repeat rhymes.) The players take turns as described until they reach Clown Town.

Flip Strip

This sorting activity is easy to modify for different skill levels!

Easier version: Ask each child to color and cut out a copy of the cards from page 217. Instruct him to put the starred cards side by side on a 3" x 12" paper strip. Then have him stack the remaining cards on the starred cards with the matching rhymes. Staple each stack at the top.

More advanced version: Make one copy of page 217, mask the stars, and then make a copy for each child. Have each youngster color and cut out the cards and then sort the cards by the corresponding rhymes. Instruct him to stack each resulting group of cards side by side on a 3" x 12" paper strip. Then staple each stack at the top.

Karen Almond, Royston Elementary, Royston, GA

Card Bonus

Here's another great way to use the cards on page 217. Display three picture cards at a time, two whose names rhyme and one whose name does not rhyme. Have students identify the rhyming pair.

Rhyme rover, rhyme rover, send Lexi right over!

Winning Pairs

This version of Red Rover is sure to please! Gather a class supply of rhyming picture cards with one rhyming match per card. Separate the rhyming pairs to make two sets of cards. Divide students into two equal-size groups and have them stand as in the traditional game. Distribute a set of cards to each group and have each youngster hold a card in clear view.

To begin, Group 1 calls out the command shown, substituting the name of a cardholder in Group 2. The named student identifies the picture on her card, quickly goes to Group 1, and finds the youngster with the matching rhyming card. Then she rushes back to Group 2 with him and they set their cards down. Next, Group 2 calls a player as described. Play continues in this manner until all the cards have been set down.

Randi Austin, Lebanon, MO

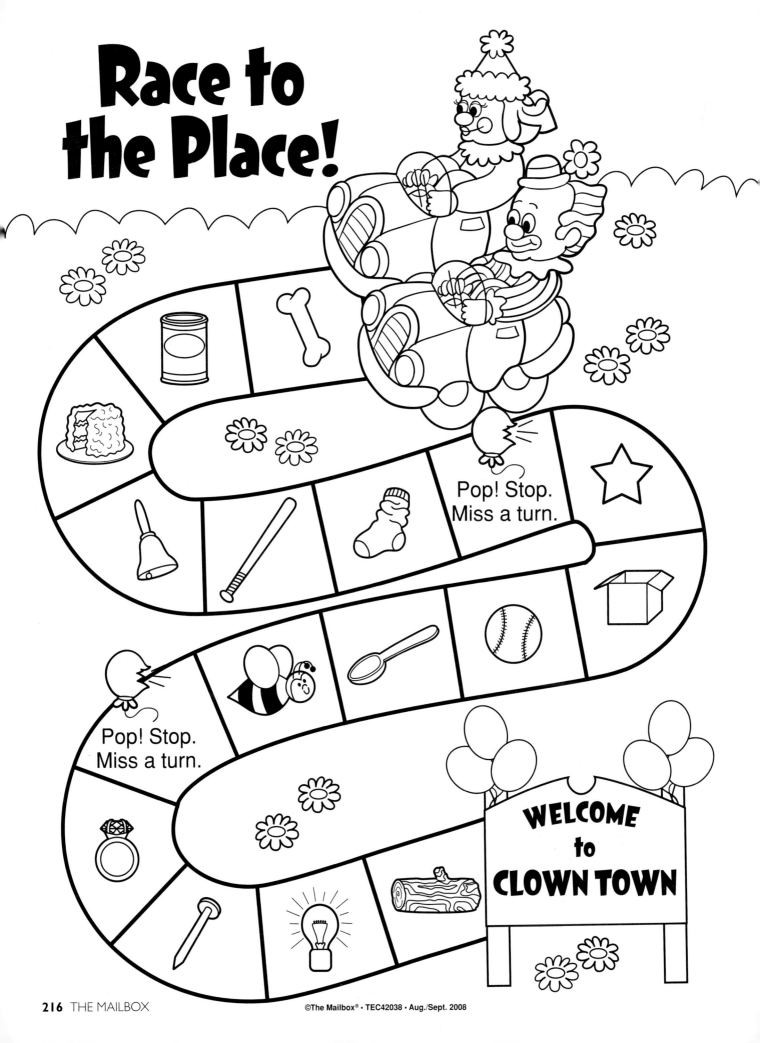

Race to the Place!

Pop! Stop.
Miss a turn.

Pop! Stop.
Miss a turn.

WELCOME
to
CLOWN TOWN

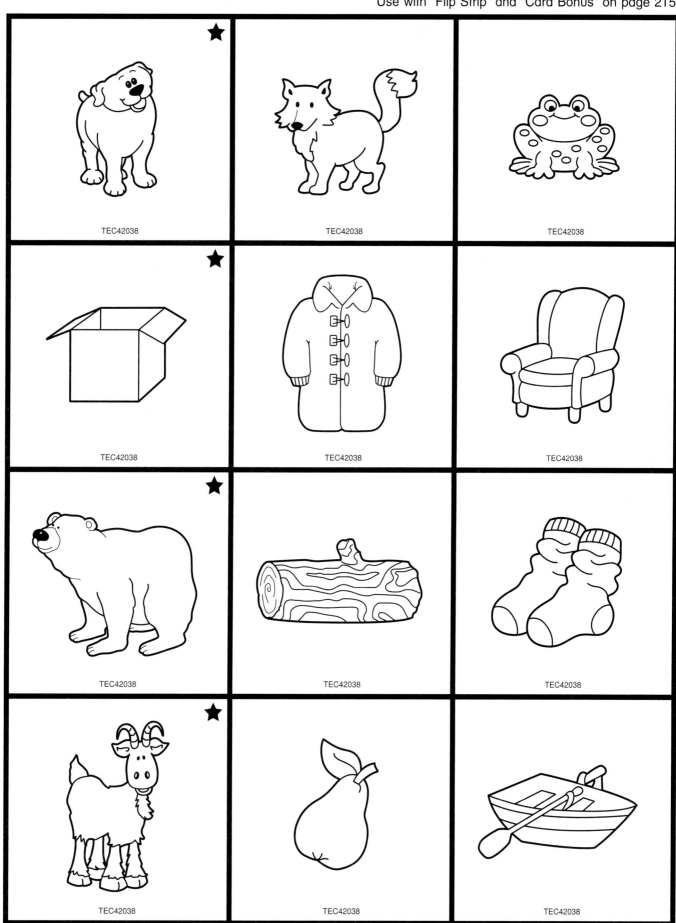

TEC42038

TEC42038

TEC42038

TEC42038

TEC42038

TEC42038

TEC42038

TEC42038

TEC42038

TEC42038

TEC42038

TEC42038

Hold Tight!

Name the pictures.

Color the balloons by the code.

Color Code
rhyme—yellow
do not rhyme—orange

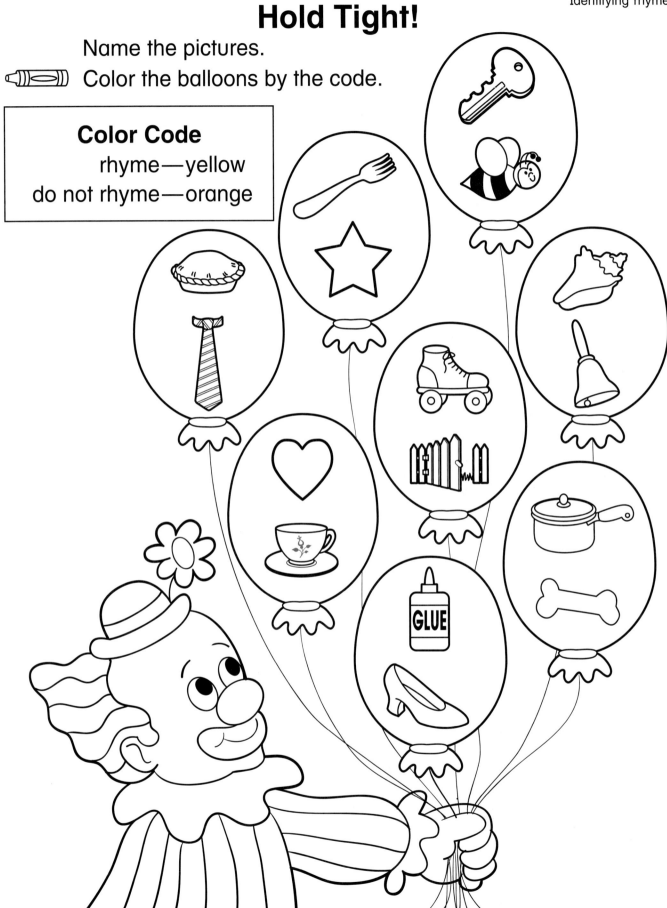

It's Time for Journals!

Spark students' enthusiasm for writing with these creative ideas.

Lovable Ideas
Choosing writing topics

What's a simple way to get students on the "write" track? Help them choose topics that are near and dear to their hearts! Give each child a copy of page 221. Have him illustrate each section of the heart to match the text, and encourage him to label his artwork. Invite him to color the rest of the paper and then instruct him to put it in his journal. When it's time for students to write, ask each youngster to refer to his paper for writing ideas or designate a chosen section of the heart and have students write about the corresponding topic.

Amy Rodriguez, P. S. 212, Brooklyn, NY

Photos and Such
Choosing writing topics

If a picture is worth a thousand words, these scrapbook pages are sure to give young writers lots to write about! Send a colorful sheet of paper home with each student along with a note asking an adult to help the youngster make a scrapbook page that shows people, activities, and occasions that are important to the child. (Explain that the scrapbook page will be returned.) After the youngster completes the page, have her return it to school. Put each child's scrapbook page in a separate top-loading page protector and then ask her to keep it in her writing folder for inspiration. To keep students' writing ideas fresh, have each youngster and a family member make a different scrapbook page each season.

Audrey Vohs, Homestead-Wakefield Elementary, Bel Air, MD

Ready Reference
Using an alphabet chart

To make this letter-perfect writing tool, list the uppercase and lowercase alphabet letters on a vertical half sheet of paper, leaving at least one inch blank at the bottom. Attach a colorful copy of the list to the back cover of each child's journal, as shown, and then fold down the list. When a child is ready to write in the journal, he unfolds the list and turns to the first blank journal page. He refers to the list as needed for help with letter formation. When he is finished writing, he folds the list down.

Bernadette Todaro, Grand Island, NY

Good Morning!
Writing to communicate

Since students often arrive at school eager to share news, why not channel that enthusiasm into writing? For each student, make a good morning journal by stapling several sheets of writing paper between two sheets of construction paper. Personalize the front cover and decorate it with a sun cutout or illustration. At the beginning of each day, have each youngster make an entry in her journal. At the end of the writing time, arrange for pairs or small groups of students to sit together and greet one another. Then invite them to share their journal entries. There's no doubt it will promote purposeful writing and build a positive classroom community!

Tina Buckley, Theodore Roosevelt School, Buffalo, NY

Tuneful Reminders
Establishing a writing community

Start your writing time with this pride-boosting song.

(sung to the tune of "I've Been Working on the Railroad")

I'm a kindergarten writer here at school today.
I'm a kindergarten writer; I have so much to say!
I can choose a good topic—
A topic just right for me.
I can draw and write great stories.
Take a look and see!

adapted from an idea by Kathy Brand
Cornerstone Christian School
New City, NY

What Can I Write About?

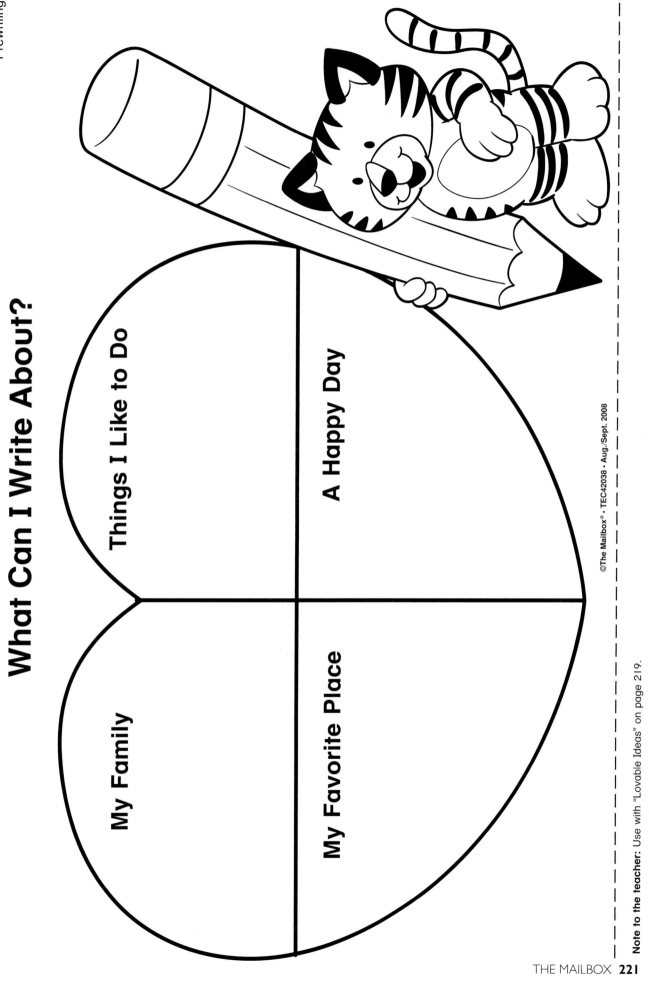

Things I Like to Do

My Family

A Happy Day

My Favorite Place

Note to the teacher: Use with "Lovable Ideas" on page 219.

Letter-Perfect Ideas

Switch!
Letter recognition

For this fun-filled game, gather a supply of matching uppercase and lowercase letter cards so there is one card per student. Have students arrange their chairs in a circle and sit down. Give each student a card at random. To play one round, name a letter. Then lead students in the song shown and have the two students with the named letter try to change places before the end of the song. For added fun, every few rounds say, "Alphabet soup!" instead of a letter. Then have all the students switch places as you sing the song, changing the first, second, and fourth lines to "If you have a letter card."

adapted from an idea by Linda Gordetsky
Boynton Creek Elementary
Delray Beach, FL

(sung to the tune of
"The Farmer in the Dell")

If you have the letter [*F*],
If you have the letter [*F*],
Change your seats; you must be quick
If you have the letter [*F*].

On the Lookout
Letter recognition

This letter-hunt activity is easy to adapt for different skill levels! In advance, gather one uppercase letter card per student. Post the cards around the room within students' reach. To begin, give each youngster a lowercase letter card that corresponds with a posted letter. Then instruct each student to look around the room for the card that matches her card. When she finds it, ask her to take the pair of cards to your large-group area and sit down. After each child is seated, have each youngster, in turn, show her cards to the group and name the corresponding letter.

For an easier version, post fewer different letters, repeating letters as needed.

For a more advanced version, instead of uppercase letter cards, post picture cards. Have each youngster find the picture whose name begins with the letter on her card.

Marlene Borysiak, Weston Elementary, Schofield, WI

Wipe Away Errors

Handwriting

Try this confidence-building idea whenever you teach students how to write a different letter. After you model the correct letter formation, give each student a handwriting paper in a plastic page protector. Then have him complete the paper with a wipe-off marker. Since the wipe-off format allows him to erase his writing, it's sure to alleviate any concerns he has about making mistakes. Plus, it allows for repeated practice. When the youngster is ready to complete the paper with a pencil, simply remove it from the page protector.

Jana Murphy, Primavera School, Prescott, AZ

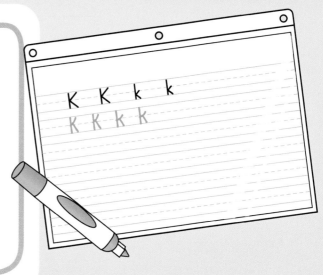

Full Steam Ahead!

Letter recognition, handwriting

This center is just the ticket for reinforcing your choice of letters. Make one copy of page 224. Write a different letter on each train engine. Then place student copies of the paper at a center along with old magazines, scissors, glue, letter stampers, and ink pads. When a youngster visits the center, she cuts from the magazines one or two examples of each featured letter and glues them on the appropriate train cars. Then she stamps and writes the letters where indicated.

Angie Kutzer, Garrett Elementary, Mebane, NC

Artsy Alphabet

Letter-sound associations

Here's a fun way to incorporate literacy into your art center. Draw a large block letter on a sheet of paper. Arrange for each student to decorate a copy of the letter with illustrations or items whose names begin with the letter. For example, you might have students make red fingerprint apples on the letter *A*, illustrate balloons on the letter *B*, make corncob paint prints on the letter *C*, and make dots with a bingo dauber on the letter *D*.

If desired, have each youngster complete a paper as described for each letter of the alphabet. Then bind his papers in alphabetical order between two covers. No doubt he'll enjoy reviewing the pages and recalling how he decorated them! **For more advanced students,** ask each youngster to write captions with the letters and corresponding words.

Deborah Provencher, West Brookfield Elementary
West Brookfield, MA

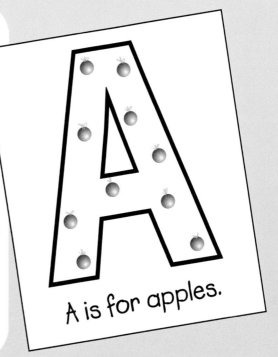

A is for apples.

Full Steam Ahead!

Write.

Stamp.

Cut and glue.

GLUE

©The Mailbox® • TEC42039 • Oct./Nov. 2008

Note to the teacher: Use with "Full Steam Ahead!" on page 223.

Custom-Made for Literacy

Build your students' reading and writing skills with these ideas.

That Was Fun!

Writing about a personal experience

Use this supersimple idea to help youngsters choose writing topics. Have each child think of a fun experience she had with a friend. Ask her to give you a thumbs-up when she pictures the experience in her mind. After she signals you in this manner, give her a copy of page 227. Have her illustrate the experience and then write about it, using additional paper if necessary.

Under Construction

Word families

Try this creative approach to sorting words! For a small group, gather three white cards (foundations), a supply of colored cards (walls), and three triangles (roofs). Write a different rime on each roof. Write a key word for each rime on a separate white card. Program each colored card with a word that contains a featured rime, programming a different number of cards for each rime. To complete the activity, the youngsters spread out the white cards to "set" the foundations. After they finish building the houses as shown, they read each group of words. Then each youngster lists on provided paper the words from the tallest house.

For an initial consonant variation, write a consonant on each white card and leave the roofs blank. Program each colored card with a picture whose name begins with a featured consonant.

Shellie Miller, Cessna Elementary, Wichita, KS

Brick by Brick

Concepts about print or word order

For these pocket-chart ideas, program red rectangles (bricks) with sentences, writing each word and any punctuation on a separate brick.

Concepts about print: Display the sentences, leaving space between the words to help students develop one-to-one correspondence between oral and written words. Have youngsters take turns wearing a pair of work gloves and pointing to the words as students read them.

Word order: Instruct students to "build" a wall by using the bricks to form sentences in separate rows of a pocket chart, beginning with the bottom row.

Shellie Miller, Cessna Elementary, Wichita, KS

Punctuation Playhouse

End marks

To prepare this variation of lotto, have each child color a copy of page 228. Then instruct him to cut out the punctuation cards and glue them on the grid in random order. Give each player eight counters to use as game markers. To play one round, display a sentence without ending punctuation and read it aloud. Ask a volunteer to identify the correct punctuation and add it to the sentence. Then have each player put a counter on a corresponding card on his gameboard. Continue as described until one or more players marks four cards in a row. **For an easier version,** use punctuated sentences. Have students point out and identify the ending punctuation before marking their gameboards.

adapted from an idea by Shellie Miller

Home Base

Initial or final consonants

Here's a lively phonics activity! Make six or more house cutouts and then write a consonant on each house. Arrange the houses in a large circle on the floor. To begin, instruct students to walk around the circle as you play some music. After a few moments, stop the music and have each youngster go to the house that is closest to him. Next, say a word. Have students identify either the initial or final consonant. Then ask each youngster at the house with the named letter to sit out the next round. Resume the music to continue.

Shellie Miller

That Was Fun!

Think about a fun time you had with a friend.

Draw a picture.

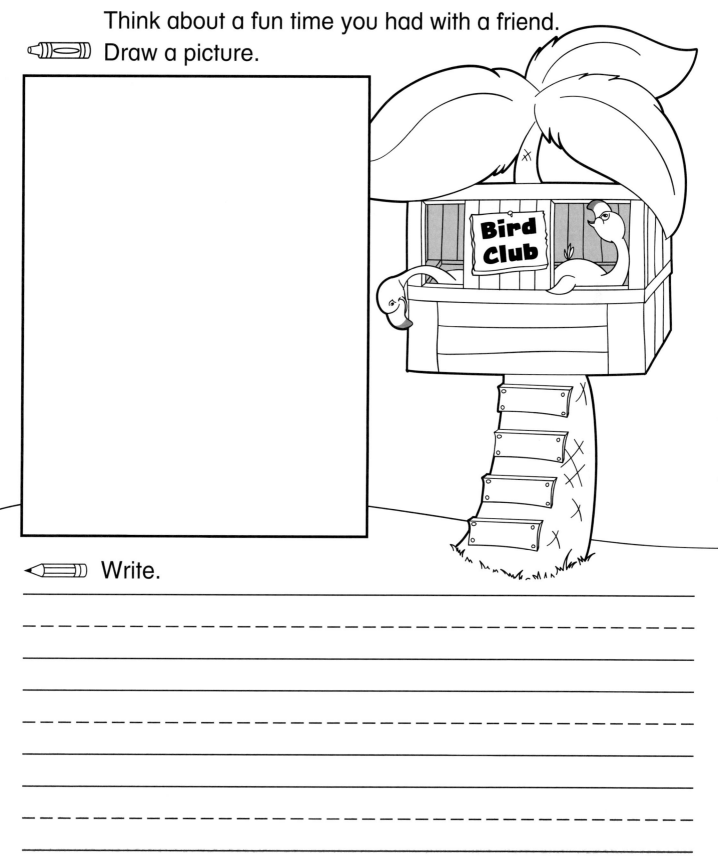

Write.

Note to the teacher: Use with "That Was Fun!" on page 225.

Punctuation Playhouse

For Writers

•

•

•

?

?

?

!

!

!

Note to the teacher: Use with "Punctuation Playhouse" on page 226.

Fresh Ideas for High-Frequency Words

How Tempting!

A popcorn-themed display is perfect to reinforce words that often pop up in students' reading and writing. To make a display, post a large popcorn tub cutout labeled as shown. Set out a marker and a supply of popcorn cutouts in a clean and empty popcorn container. Whenever you introduce a high-frequency word to students, write it on a cutout and add it to the display. At a chosen time each day, declare a popcorn break and review the words with students.

Kendra Wilson
Windsor Elementary
Columbia, SC

Like Royalty

To make a crown for each student, write a chosen word on a sentence strip cut as shown. Trace the word with glitter glue and allow the glue to dry. Then size the strip to the child's head and secure the ends. After each child has a crown, schedule a Royal Word Day. On the designated day, instead of having students call one another by name, encourage them to say *Prince* or *Princess* and the word on the appropriate youngster's crown. Use the crowns and the ideas below for more fun-filled skill practice.

Royal Writing: Give each youngster a sheet of paper. Have him pair up with different classmates to read and write their assigned words.

King's Court: Ask a few students to stand side by side. Point to the word on each crown, in turn, and have the seated students read it. Then direct students to read the words faster and in random order.

Majestic Sentences: Post a large castle cutout within students' reach. Ask each student to dictate a sentence with his word. Write the sentence on the castle and then invite the youngster to circle the featured word.

adapted from an idea by Jeanne Cruz
Hualapai Elementary
Kingman, AZ

Music and Movement

This variation of musical chairs not only helps little ones get the wiggles out but also gives them practice reading your word wall. Put on each child's desk or table space a card with the number 1, 2, 3, or 4. Next, instruct students to walk in a path around all the desks or tables as you play some music. After a few moments, stop the music and have each child sit at the nearest empty seat. Then call out a number from 1 to 4 and ask each child at a seat with a matching card to stand and read a chosen word. To continue play, instruct all the students to stand; then resume the music.

Maureen Behrs, Tam Valley Elementary, Mill Valley, CA

Simple Sentences

For this small-group activity, have each child cut out a copy of the sentence cards from page 231. Next, say a sentence that can be formed with the cards. Ask each youngster to arrange her cards accordingly and punctuate the resulting sentence. After you help students make any needed corrections, say a different sentence for them to form.

For a variation, make an overhead transparency of page 231 and cut apart the cards. Set up an overhead projector at a learning center. Have center visitors form sentences on the projector and write them on paper.

Katie Zuehlke, Bendix Elementary, Annandale, MN

Stepping Ahead

Once you prepare this activity, you can use it again and again! Make a class supply of footprint cutouts. Write a chosen word on each footprint and laminate the footprints for durability. Then arrange the footprints on the floor in a path to the door. Whenever individual students leave the room, encourage them to walk along the path and read the words as they go. For additional practice, make flash cards with the same words. When it's time for students to line up, have each youngster, in turn, read a card, find the matching footprint, and then stand beside it.

Melanie Guido
St. Francis-St. Stephen School
Geneva, NY

like	! .	cat	bat
see	and	dog	pig
have	a	one	rat
I	a	the	bug

TEC42040

Word Family Fun

Out the Door
Naming words

Make naming word family words part of your daily routine. Designate one student each week to be the word keeper. (It works well to have the door holder take on this job.) Have the word keeper stand at the door and wear a tagboard necklace with a rime on it. As each student walks out the door, she quietly announces a word in the word family.

Amber Hodge, Annoor Academy, Knoxville, TN

Open It!
Reading word families

Use and reuse this poster to introduce new word families. On a half sheet of poster board, draw a simple schoolhouse outline; then laminate the poster. Using a wipe-off marker, label the top of the poster with a rime and an illustration of a word in that family. For each word you would like to introduce, add details to the schoolhouse using sticky notes made to look like several windows and a door. Attach the windows and door to the poster. Then lift each sticky note and write a word family word underneath.

Introduce the rime and the key picture. Explain that all the words on the school are in the same word family, so they all have the same rime. Then recite the chant shown. At the end of the verse, invite a child to lift a window or door and read the word aloud. Continue until each word has been read.

Carolyn S. Kanoy, Julian Gibson Elementary, Winston-Salem, NC

Open a window
Or open the door.
Now read a word
We haven't read before!

Full Houses
Sorting words

Write each of two rimes on triangle shapes (roofs). Then program each of several cards with a different word that has one of the rimes. Place the roofs at the top of a pocket chart. Give a child a card and have her place it under the appropriate roof. Ask the class to identify the word family, read the word, and verify the placement of the card. Continue with each card to make two full houses.

adapted from an idea by Katy Hoh, W. C. K. Walls Elementary
Pitman, NJ

Write On, Wipe Off
Making words

The result of this center is a handy word family reference. Write a rime at the top of a sheet of chart paper. Then rewrite the rime for each word that can be formed with a single consonant, leaving a blank for the onset. After laminating the chart, place it at a center with wipe-off markers and consonant letter cards. A child adds a letter card to the rime, and if it makes a word, he writes the letter on the chart. He continues until each word is made. After checking the chart, wipe off the writing to prepare for the next student. When all students have visited the center, post the completed chart as a reference.

Amy Rodriguez, Public School 212, Brooklyn, NY

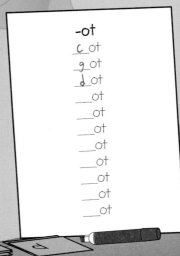

Sing and Write
Writing words

Help students read and write words with this catchy tune. Write a rime on the board. Then write onsets that can be used to make words with that rime. To begin, invite a student to stand near the board and give her a marker. Lead youngsters in the song shown, inserting the rime, the child's name, and a word where indicated. At the end of the song, have the child with the marker choose the correct onset and write the word on the board. Cross out the used onset and play again.

Kathryn Keiter, Bonsack Elementary, Roanoke, VA

(sung to the tune of "London Bridge")

We know words to make with [-ug],
Make with [-ug], make with [-ug].
We know words to make with [-ug];
[Child's name], write [rug]!

Wild About Words
Writing words

This nifty reproducible can be used for practice with any word family. Program the speech bubble on a copy of page 234 with a word family word. Then write on the roof several letters, some that make other words in that word family and some that do not. Copy the page to make a class supply. A student uses the letters on the roof to help him write words in the same word family as the one in the speech bubble.

Jennifer Goldman, Sol Feinstone Elementary, Newtown, PA

Jungle House

✏ Write words.
Use the letters to help you.

If I can spell
_____, then
I can spell...

Note to the teacher: Use with "Wild About Words" on page 233.

Have each child cut out a copy of the onset and rime cards and the word list below. Instruct him to form words with the cards, read the words, and then write them on paper. Invite him to take the cards and word list home in an envelope for practice. If desired, follow up with the activity on page 236.

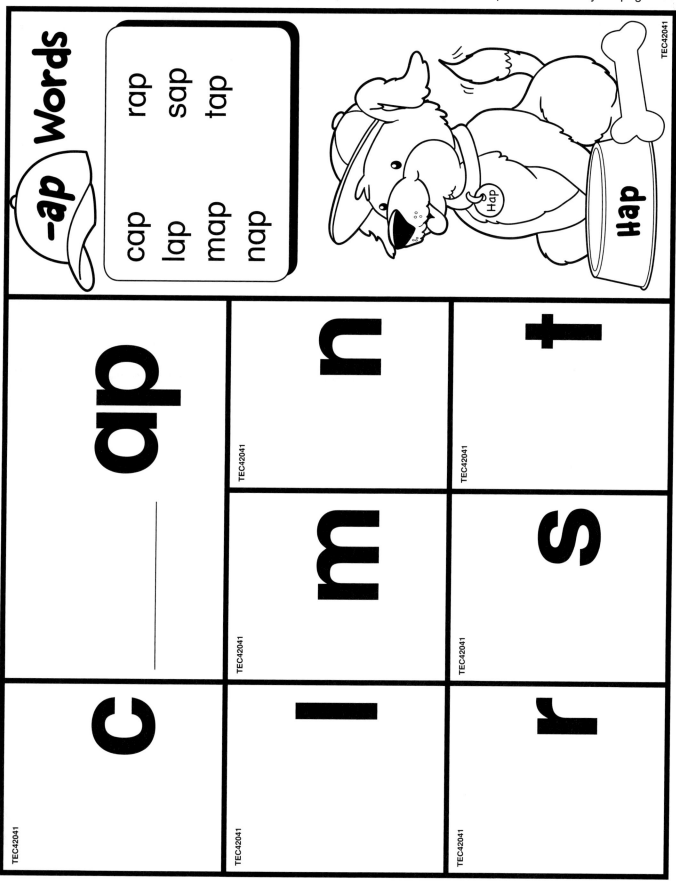

-ap Words

rap	cap
sap	lap
tap	map
	nap

TEC42041

Hap

Hap

ap

n

t

_____

m

s

c

l

r

TEC42041

TEC42041

TEC42041

TEC42041

TEC42041

TEC42041

Name _____ Word family: -ap

My Dog, Hap

Cut.

Glue.

1. My dog has a  .

2. My dog has a .

3. My dog likes my .

4. My dog likes to !

| map | nap | cap | lap |

Hop Into Reading

Shop.

Music and Motion
Word family -op

To prepare, teach youngsters the moves to the tune "The Bunny Hop." When students are comfortable with the motions, stop the music at the end of each verse to have a child name a word in the -op word family. Write each word on the board. To review, have youngsters hop in place as you read the list of words together.

Sheri Ollar
Cottonwood Creek Elementary
Coppell, TX

Carrots

Carrots for Bunnies!
Skill review

Cut out a class supply of the carrot pattern on page 239 for these lively whole-group options.

Letter-sound association: Program the carrots with individual letters. Give each youngster a carrot. Then say the sound for a letter. Encourage each student with that letter to hop like a bunny. Continue with different sounds until each little bunny has had a turn.

Initial or final consonants: Program the carrots with consonants. Give each youngster a carrot. Announce whether you are looking for the initial or final consonant and then say a word. Have each child with that beginning or ending letter hop like a bunny.

Counting syllables in words: Program the carrots with animal stickers whose names have one, two, or three syllables. Label different areas in your room "1," "2," and "3." To begin, give each youngster a carrot. Have him name the animal and count the number of syllables. On your signal, have each child hop to the corresponding area of the room.

Katie Zuehlke
Bendix Elementary
Annandale, MN

To Hop or Not
Beginning and ending sounds

For this class activity, designate half your class to listen for beginning sounds and the other half to listen for ending sounds. Announce a sound. Then say a word that begins or ends with that sound. A child hops if he hears the sound in his designated location (at the beginning or end of a word).

Who Gets the Carrot?
Word families

At this sorting center, youngsters pretend to feed hungry bunnies. Program a copy of the recording sheet on page 239 with two different rimes and make a class supply. Then write on several carrot cutouts (pattern on page 239) words for each rime. Place the carrots and recording sheets at a center. A student sorts the carrots by word family. Then she writes each word by the corresponding carrot on her recording sheet. **For an easier version,** program the recording sheet with the words from the carrots. Have youngsters match the word on each carrot to a word on the paper and color the corresponding bunny.

adapted from an idea by Katie Zuehlke
Bendix Elementary
Annandale, MN

Read That Word!
High-frequency words

For this center activity, post a list of words to review. Write each word on an individual carrot cutout (pattern on page 239) and place the carrots in a bag. A youngster copies each word from the list on a sheet of paper. Then she removes a carrot, reads the word, and makes a tally mark next to the matching word on her paper. She returns the carrot to the bag and continues with more carrots until one word has a total of ten tally marks.

adapted from an idea by Katie Zuchlke

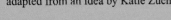

Name_____

Who Gets the Carrot?

Follow your teacher's directions.

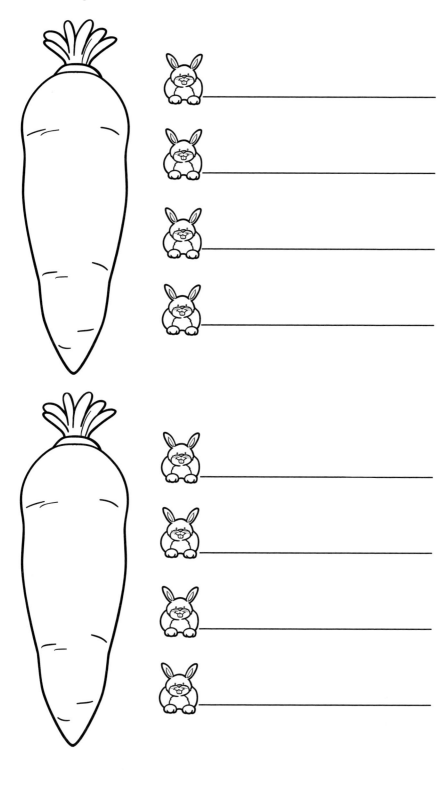

Note to the teacher: Use with "Who Gets the Carrot?" on page 238.

Carrot Pattern
Use with "Carrots for Bunnies!" on page 237 and "Who Gets the Carrot?" and "Read That Word!" on page 238.

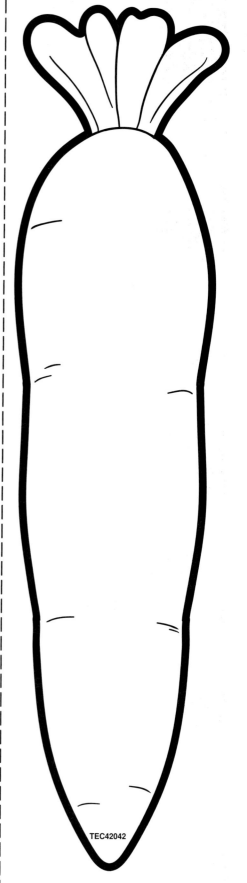

TEC42042

Cool Letter Review

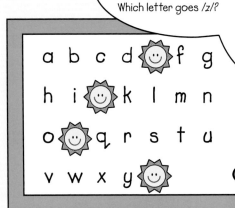

Which letter is after *d?*
Which letter is before *q?*
Which letter does *jump* begin with?
Which letter goes /z/?

Alphabet Mats

This activity can be used again and again for almost any letter skill or as an assessment! For each child, prepare a letter mat similar to the one shown. Then have youngsters respond to letter- and sound-related questions by placing a seasonal eraser, manipulative, or counter on the correct answer.

Kim Criswell, Wilson, KS

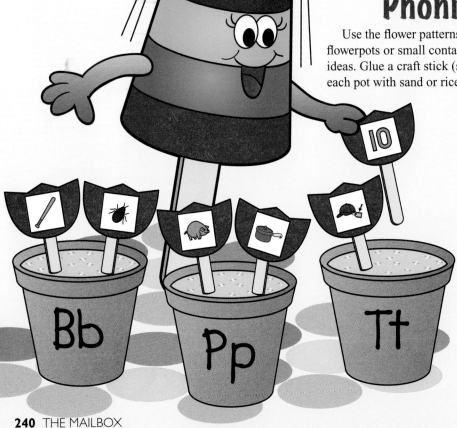

Phonics Flowerpots

Use the flower patterns and picture cards on page 242 and six plastic flowerpots or small containers to prepare for these manipulative center ideas. Glue a craft stick (stem) to each prepared flower and partially fill each pot with sand or rice. Then choose a skill below.

Letter matching: Label each flowerpot with a different matching letter pair. Program the flowers with individual letters that match the flowerpots. A youngster puts each flower in the matching flowerpot.

Beginning consonants: Label each flowerpot with one of the following letters: *b, h, n, p, s,* and *t.* Glue each picture card to a separate flower. A child names each picture, identifies the beginning letter, and puts the flower in the matching flowerpot.

Ending consonants: Label each flowerpot with one of the following letters: *d, g, m, n, p,* and *t.* Glue each picture card to a separate flower. A child names each picture, identifies the ending letter, and puts the flower in the matching flowerpot.

Sarah Huntley, Kelleytown Baptist Kindergarten Hartsville, SC

The ABCs of Kindergarten

Students are sure to strike a pose with this letter review! Invite two youngsters to use their bodies to each mimic a form of the same letter; then take a photograph. Brainstorm with students different words that begin with the letter and then post the picture with the corresponding words. Continue with different poses to display letters from *A* to *Z*.

Laura Olivera, St. Charles School
Bloomington, IN

rhyme
read
Rita
run

Dog.

Doughnut.

Dinosaur.

The mystery letter is *D!*

Name That Letter!

Student-given clues solve this mystery game! Invite a child to be a letter detective and have him stand in the front of the room. Then secretly show the rest of the group a desired letter. Classmates give clues, such as words that begin with the letter, until the detective correctly names the mystery letter.

Marie E. Cecchini, West Dundee, IL

What's Missing?

This partner center reviews letter names and provides practice with CVC words. Place in each of several bags a different CVC picture word card with the matching letter manipulatives. A pair takes a bag, reads the word, and uses the letters to spell the word. Next, one student secretly removes a letter and the word card, and his partner names the missing letter. If his partner needs help, he shows the word card. Players continue as time permits, switching roles each round.

adapted from an idea by Jody Carlson, Smith Elementary, Berea, OH

cat

Flower Patterns and Picture Cards
Use with "Phonics Flowerpots" on page 240.

TEC42043

TEC42043

TEC42043

TEC42043

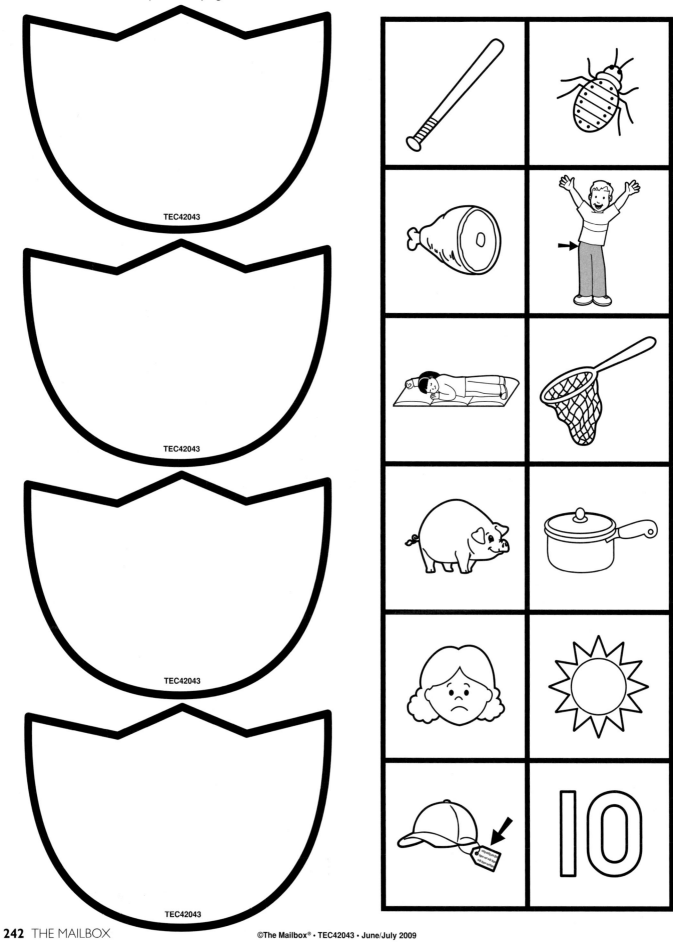

LITERATURE UNITS

Froggy Goes to School

Written by Jonathan London
Illustrated by Frank Remkiewicz

Froggy is so worried he will be late his first day of school that he dreams he gets on the bus wearing only underwear! Fortunately, the day begins much more smoothly than Froggy imagines and leaves him in high spirits.

ideas contributed by Ada Goren
Winston-Salem, NC

Flop, Flop, Flop!

Participating in a read-aloud

Engage your students in this "sound-sational" story by having them make sound effects! After a first reading, hold an index card in each hand, keeping one end of each card free. Flap the free ends of the cards against one another to imitate the sound Froggy makes when he walks. Next, give each youngster two index cards and invite students to practice flapping their cards together as you did. Then reread the book, prompting students to make the demonstrated sound whenever Froggy walks. For added fun, have students imitate Miss Witherspoon's clapping at the appropriate point in the story.

Flop!

Flop!

I ride in a car.   Betsy

Froggy rides a bus to school.
He thinks learning is really cool!

Getting There

Reading a predictable book

Whether or not your students ride a bus to school as Froggy does, count on this class book to get them on the road to reading! To prepare, make a supply of transportation cards (patterns on page 246).

Have each youngster color a transportation card that represents how she usually gets to school. Instruct her to incorporate the card into an illustration on a horizontal sheet of paper. As students work, invite each youngster, in turn, to dictate a sentence similar to the one shown to match her illustration. Write the sentence and her name on her paper. To make the last page of the class book, program a sheet of paper with the Froggy-related sentences shown and have a volunteer illustrate them. Then stack students' completed papers on the last page. Bind the stack between two covers and title the resulting book "Going to School." The picture clues and predictable format are sure to build students' confidence in reading!

Hop to It!

Story recall

Careful listeners are bound to learn a lot about Froggy and his family. To recap the information, bring in a toy stuffed frog or decorate a green beanbag to look like a frog face. Sit with students in a circle. Then have the frog "hop" to a youngster by gently tossing it to the student. After the child tells the group one thing he learned from the story about Froggy or his family, instruct him to toss the frog back to you. Continue as described, encouraging students not to repeat previously shared information, until each youngster has had a turn.

Hop, hop, hop.

Where will
Reading Frog stop?

Wonderful Words

Reading names

Froggy adores his nametag. After all, it shows the only word he knows how to read! Help your students read lots of words with this pocket chart name activity. Write each student's name on a separate blank card. Display several cards in a pocket chart. Color and cut out a copy of the frog pattern on page 246. Then attach it to one end of a ruler or craft stick to make a pointer. To play one round, point to different name cards as you say the chant shown. When you say the last word in the chant, stop moving the pointer and keep it directed to a chosen card. Then have students read the corresponding name. To continue, invite the named student to use the pointer as described as you lead the class in saying the chant. Substitute different name cards as needed to ensure that each youngster's name is displayed during at least one round.

Summer Reflections

Responding to literature

Froggy and his classmates had fun during the summer and no doubt your students did too! After students recall what Froggy did in the summer, have volunteers tell the class about their summer activities. Then give each youngster a large blank index card and a slightly larger yellow circle. Have her illustrate on the card an activity she enjoyed during the summer. Help her add a caption and glue the card to the circle. Then ask her to glue yellow crepe paper streamers to the back of the circle to make sun rays. Display students' completed work with the title "Bright Vacations."

I saw my grandma.

Transportation Cards

Use with "Getting There" on page 244.

TEC42038

TEC42038

TEC42038

TEC42038

TEC42038

Frog Pattern

Use with "Wonderful Words" on page 245.

©The Mailbox® • TEC42038 • Aug./Sept. 2008

Tacky the Penguin

by Helen Lester

Tacky the penguin is not like his penguin companions. He does not march like them, dive like them, or even sing like them. But it is his unique personality that deters a group of penguin hunters from trapping his friends and him. In the end of this humorous tale, the other penguins realize that even though Tacky is different, he is a very important friend.

ideas contributed by Ada Goren, Winston-Salem, NC

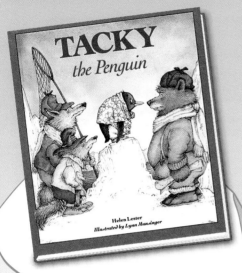

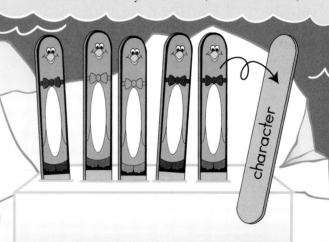

Pick a Penguin

Story elements

Add an arctic twist to reviewing the important parts of the story. After youngsters are familiar with the story, glue five copies of the penguin pattern (page 248) to separate large craft sticks. Program the back of each stick with one of the following story elements: *character, setting, event from the beginning, event from the middle,* and *event from the end.* Insert the penguins into a block of white foam or a container filled with rice to make an iceberg. Invite a child to pick a penguin from the iceberg and help him read the stick. Then ask youngsters to identify that story element. After accepting several answers, put the penguin aside and continue with the remaining penguins.

An Extraordinary Bird

Reality and fantasy

Youngsters are sure to find the fantastical things that Tacky does to be entertaining! Guide students to understand that Tacky is a character in a story and does not act like a real penguin. Then help each child fold a 9" x 12" sheet of paper in half and unfold it. Have her cut out a copy of the reality and fantasy penguin cards and strips on page 248. Direct her to glue each penguin card to the top of a different column on her paper. Then help her read each strip and glue it in the correct column.

So Special!

Story theme

Tacky is not like his friends, which is why he is unique! After reading the story, ask students to name some things that Tacky does that are different from what his companions do. Lead little ones to conclude that everyone is special in her own way. Then give each child two shirt cutouts. Have her decorate one shirt as desired. On the other shirt, encourage her to draw, write, or dictate something special about herself. To complete the project, help her place the decorated shirt atop the other shirt and staple them together as shown. Then help her cut through the middle of the top shirt. Encourage each child to share her unique project with the class.

Penguin Patterns
Use with "Pick a Penguin" on page 247.

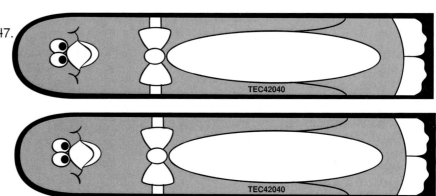

Reality and Fantasy Penguin Cards and Strips
Use with "An Extraordinary Bird" on page 247.

©The Mailbox® • TEC42040 • Dec./Jan. 2008–9

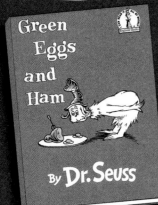

Green Eggs and Ham

Written and illustrated by Dr. Seuss

Do you like green eggs and ham? When Sam poses this question, it triggers a series of outlandish events designed to tempt the main character to try this colorful cuisine!

ideas contributed by Ada Goren, Winston-Salem, NC

We Would Try Them!

Rhyming words

Students play the role of Sam in this engaging class book. Have each youngster draw green eggs and ham on a paper plate. Then photograph each child holding his plate. Have him attach his photo to a sheet of paper programmed as shown. Then prompt him to name two rhyming words and write them in the spaces provided. Bind the completed pages together with a cover to make an "egg-cellent" class book!

Yuck or Yum?

Writing, speaking to express an opinion

No doubt youngsters have tried new foods just as the main character in the story did! Encourage each child to think of a time when she has tasted a new food. Encourage her to draw on a copy of page 250 a picture of herself eating the food. Have her write the food name on her paper and then add an X to one of the boxes to express her opinion of the food. Encourage each child to share her paper with the class, naming the food she tasted and whether she found the food to her liking.

I ate _____

_____ .

😊 I liked it! ☐   ☹ I did not like it! ☐

©The Mailbox® • TEC42041 • Feb./Mar. 2009

250 THE MAILBOX   **Note to the teacher:** Use with "Yuck or Yum?" on page 249.

THE GIGANTIC TURNIP

Written by Aleksei Tolstoy
Illustrated by Niamh Sharkey

When an old lady and an old man harvest their crops, they are surprised to discover that they have a gigantic turnip! It takes the cooperative effort of the entire household to uproot this turnip to make a huge bowl of turnip stew.

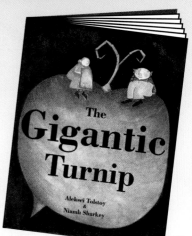

ideas contributed by Cathy Wroten
Bear Branch Elementary
Magnolia, TX

What Happens?

Predicting

What might happen in a story about a gigantic turnip? No doubt youngsters will be eager to share their predictions with this idea! Show students a real turnip and then help them name and describe this unique vegetable. Explain that your turnip is normal size but the turnip in the book you're about to read is gigantic! Ask students to predict what might happen in a book about a gigantic turnip. Then encourage youngsters to settle in for the read-aloud. When the story is finished, have youngsters discuss their predictions.

A Trio of Turnips

Identifying beginning, middle, and end

For each child, fold a 9" x 12" sheet of brown construction paper in half and staple the ends to make a pocket (garden). Prompt each youngster to write what happens in the beginning, middle, and end of the story on separate turnip cutouts (see page 252). Have him color the cutouts as desired. Then help him stack the turnips in order, staple them together, and tuck them into his garden.

The people
The people planted a garden
They tried to pull the turnip
The turnip came out

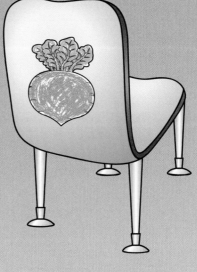

Everybody Pull!

Retelling the story

After a second reading of the story, have youngsters take part in this interactive retelling! Give each youngster a role. (Add or remove animal characters as needed to fit your class size). Attach a large turnip cutout to the back of a chair. Then help students retell and act out the story, having youngsters hold on to each other's waists as they pretend to pull the turnip.

Turnip Pattern

Use with "A Trio of Turnips" on page 251.

TEC42042

In the Tall, Tall Grass

Written and illustrated by Denise Fleming

During a caterpillar's journey through the tall, tall grass, it encounters a variety of munching, humming, flapping creatures. Denise Fleming's characteristic pulp illustrations enhance the simple text of this story.

ideas by Angie Kutzer, Garrett Elementary, Mebane, NC

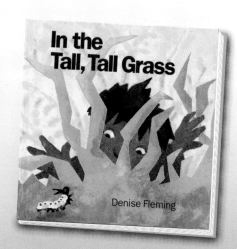

In the Tall, Tall Grass

Denise Fleming

I see 4 roks. I see a lot uv antz. Sum gras wuz brown and sum waz green.

A Circle of Grass

Writing

The caterpillar sees a variety of things in the grass. No doubt your youngsters will too! Take students outside and have each child place a circle of yarn on a patch of grass. Encourage him to study the grass inside the circle. If desired, have each child use a craft stick to gently move the grass in his area to get a better view. After returning to the classroom, have each child write on a sheet of story paper a description of what he saw and then draw a matching illustration.

Tall, Taller, Tallest

Ordering by height

With this activity, youngsters order blades of grass and then add their favorite critters from the story. Give each child several green paper strips in different lengths (grass). Have her arrange her strips in order by height on a sheet of construction paper. When the strips have been ordered correctly, encourage her to glue them in place. Finally, invite her to draw her favorite critters from the story on a separate piece of paper. Then have her cut out the critters and glue them to her project.

sun, fun, tigers run
ding, ring, birds sing
creep, sleep, frogs leap
dark, park, dogs bark
call, fall, snails crawl
bunnies hop
bears eat
cats nap
horses trot

Zap, Snap!

Rhyming

Students create rhyming words in this story follow-up. First, reread the story, pausing briefly to have youngsters identify each set of rhyming words. Next, write on chart paper a student-generated list of critters and an action word that corresponds to each one. Then have students name two words that rhyme with each action word as you write their responses in front of the animal's name. To conclude, lead youngsters in reading aloud the resulting phrases.

Looking for Legs

Cut.
Sort.
Glue.

2 legs

4 legs

6 legs

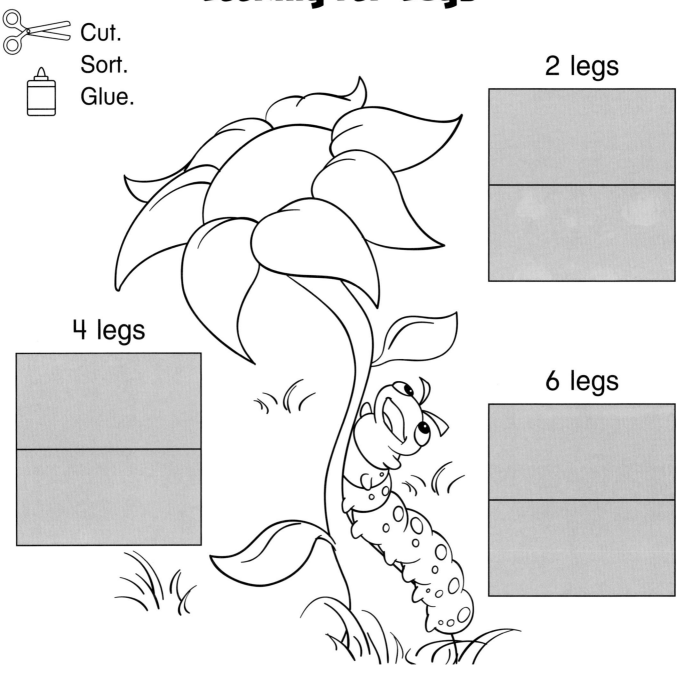

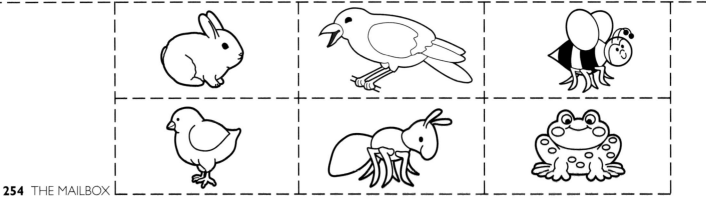

MATH UNITS

Chick Cards and Rhyme
Use with "Count Your Chicks!" on page 256.

TEC42038 TEC42038 TEC42038 TEC42038 TEC42038

TEC42038 TEC42038 TEC42038 TEC42038 TEC42038

_____ little chicks say, "Peep, peep, peep!"
number
In the henhouse they all sleep.

TEC42038

Farm Animal Cards
Use with "Farm Favorites" and "Guess the Rule!" on page 257.

TEC42038 TEC42038 TEC42038

TEC42038 TEC42038

TEC42038 TEC42038 TEC42038

Pigs in Puddles

Follow your teacher's directions.

A. ⬜ + ⬜ = ⬜

B. ⬜ + ⬜ = ⬜

C. ⬜ + ⬜ = ⬜

D. ⬜ + ⬜ = ⬜

E. ⬜ + ⬜ = ⬜

©The Mailbox® • TEC42038 • Aug./Sept. 2008

Note to the teacher: Use with "Pigs in Puddles" on page 256.

"Whoooo's" Ready for Math Fun?

Watch students' skills soar with these simple ideas.

That is the fourth owl!

"Tree-mendous" Lineup

Ordinal numbers

For this group activity, draw a long tree branch on the board within student reach. Then arrange several owl cutouts (patterns on page 262) side by side on the branch. Next, ask a volunteer to draw a designated shape above an owl of his choice. Then have him point to the owl and ask his classmates to identify the owl's ordinal position. After a youngster correctly identifies the owl's position in the bird lineup, invite her to draw a shape above a different owl. Continue as described until students have identified each bird's ordinal position.

I spy an owl near the stapler.

Where?

Positional words

Here are two more ways to use the owl patterns from page 262!

Top, Bottom, or Middle? Draw a tree on the board. Post three different-colored owls so one is at the top of the tree, one is at the middle of the tree, and one is at the bottom of the tree. Have students use the word *top, bottom,* or *middle* to describe the location of each owl. Then rearrange the owls and ask youngsters to describe the owls' new locations.

I Spy: Have each student color and cut out a copy of an owl pattern and then write her name on the back of it. Instruct students to put their owls in clear view in various places around the room. Next, invite a student to say, "I spy an owl…" and then use a positional word to describe the location of a classmate's owl. After your young birdwatchers point out the described owl, have its owner take it to her seat and then describe a different owl's location.

Angie Kutzer, Garrett Elementary, Mebane, NC

Give a Hoot!

Odd and even numbers

For student reference, display a number line on which you have marked each odd number with a sticky dot. Label an owl cutout (patterns on page 262) as shown and post it above an odd number. Randomly arrange several odd and even number cards near the number line. To begin, dim the lights. Tell students that Odd Owl lands only on odd numbers and they need to let him know which numbers are odd. Then shine a flashlight on a card. If the corresponding number is odd, the students say, "Hoot!" If the number is even, the students pantomime an owl flapping its wings. Continue with the remaining cards in the same manner.

Angie Kutzer, Garrett Elementary, Mebane, NC

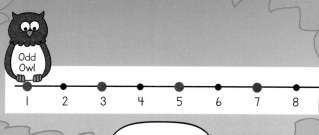

Owl and Mouse

Counting backward

Count on this variation of Duck, Duck, Goose to spark students' enthusiasm for math! Have students sit in a circle, and ask one child to be the mouse. To play one round, the mouse walks around the outside of the circle, tapping each classmate's head as she counts backward from a designated number. When she taps a child and says, "One," the tapped youngster becomes the owl and chases the mouse around the circle. If the owl tags the mouse, the mouse sits in the middle of the circle for the next round. If the mouse reaches the space where the owl was sitting without being tagged, she sits down. Then the player who is the owl becomes the mouse for the next round.

Angie Kutzer

Fine-Feathered Facts

Addition

Display several of these spotted owls to showcase math facts! To make a spotted owl, a youngster glues a circle, a large oval, and two smaller ovals together as shown. Then he adds facial details with provided arts-and-crafts supplies. Next, he puts a designated number of two-color counters in a cup and then spills them out. He records how many counters there are for each color by putting corresponding sets of sticky dots on the owl's wings. Then he writes the matching addition fact on the owl's body.

Angie Kutzer

Owl Patterns

Use with "'Tree-mendous' Lineup" and "Where?" on page 260 and "Give a Hoot!" on page 261.

TEC42039

TEC42039

Starry Night

 Write each group of numbers from the
least to the **greatest.**

A.

9
11
10

_____ , _____ , _____

B.

8
10
5

_____ , _____ , _____

C.

7
4
12

_____ , _____ , _____

D.

3
9
6

_____ , _____ , _____

E.

2
11
6

_____ , _____ , _____

F.

6
12
10

_____ , _____ , _____

Great for Graphing!

Quick and Easy

Use colored masking tape to make a blank graph on a large sheet of paper or poster board. It's faster than drawing a graph. To save even more time, laminate the graph for reuse!

Lucia Botello, Early Childhood Center, Eagle Pass, TX

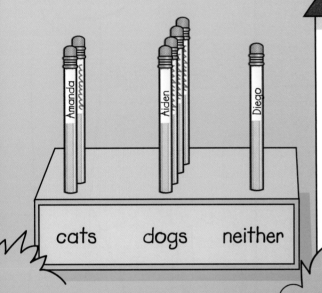

Fun Formats

Try these alternatives to traditional graphs. They're practical, creative, and just right for young learners!

Foam block: Label one side of a foam block with choices about which you would like to poll students. Have each youngster stand a personalized sharpened pencil in the block to indicate his choice. Then tilt the block to give students a clear view of the results.

Sticky notes: Instead of coloring a bar graph, instruct students to complete the graph with sticky notes.

Blocks: Have students make adjacent towers with LEGO blocks or similar blocks to make a three-dimensional bar graph.

Diana Meaney, Middle Village, NY

Day by Day

Get more skill practice out of completing a graph. Here's how! Post a blank graph for a topic about which you would like to poll students. Designate a different color for each response choice and cut a supply of matching paper squares. To begin, have each student take a paper square that corresponds with her response. Collect the squares in a paper bag. Then instruct volunteers to take a few squares from the bag and post them on the graph. Discuss the displayed data with students and pose relevant addition problems for them to solve. Continue as described over a few days until the graph is complete. No doubt students' anticipation for the results will build each day!

Jenny Lowe, Cooper Elementary, Loganville, GA

Playful Painted Mice

This literature follow-up doubles as a color-mixing idea. Read aloud *Mouse Paint* by Ellen Stoll Walsh. Next, set out red, blue, and yellow paint that you have thinned with water. Give each child a copy of the mouse pattern from page 266 and ask him to write his name on the back of it. Then instruct him to paint the front of the mouse a chosen color. Before the paint dries, have him paint the mouse a second color so the two colors mix together. Allow the paint to dry. The next day, display a graph grid like the one shown. Instruct each child to post his mouse on the grid. Then have students compare the number of mice in each column.

Vicki Altland
Florence Mattison Elementary
Conway, AR

Our Mouse Colors

Graphing in Season

Since this activity is so easy to prepare, you'll want to repeat it at different times of the year! Give each child a blank graph and a disposable cup containing seasonal confetti shapes of various colors or types. Have each youngster sort the confetti and then color the graph to show how many shapes she has of each type.

For an easier version, have her glue the confetti to the graph rather than color the graph.
For a more advanced version, ask each student to write about her completed graph.

Ruth Heckathorn, Oakland Elementary, Inman, SC

What a Harvest!

To prepare this fresh-from-the-garden activity, make copies of the vegetable cards from page 266 so there is one card for each student and the quantities of the different vegetables vary. Randomly spread the cards facedown on a large piece of brown paper (garden). Post a graph grid that you have titled and labeled as shown. Have each student, in turn, "pick" a vegetable, color the appropriate space on the graph, and put the vegetable in a basket. Once students have picked the entire crop, guide them to discuss the graph with words such as *more, fewer,* and *altogether.*

Ada Goren, Winston-Salem, NC

Our Garden Graph

Mouse Pattern
Use with "Playful Painted Mice" on page 265.

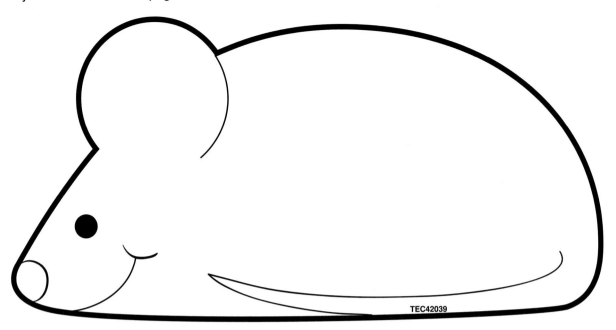

TEC42039

Vegetable Cards
Use with "What a Harvest!" on page 265.

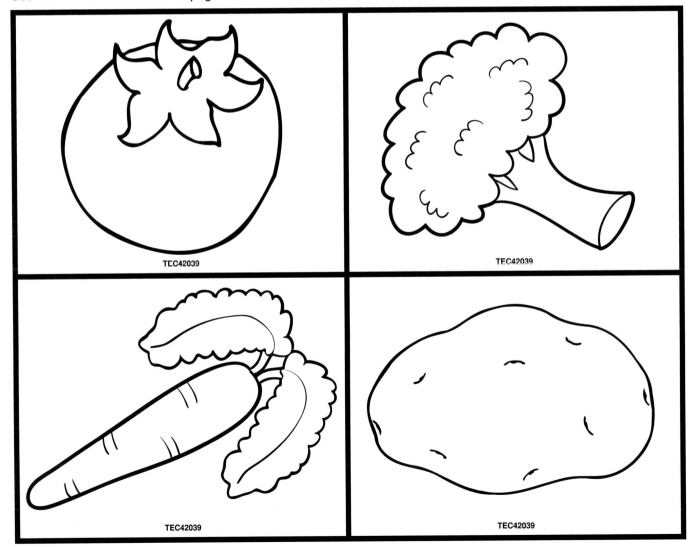

TEC42039

TEC42039

TEC42039

TEC42039

A Pocketful of Coin Ideas

This coin is the smallest one.

What's in the Pouch?

Identifying coins

This class guessing game reinforces the characteristics of coins. To play, secretly place a coin in a construction paper pouch, similar to the one shown. Then give clues about the hidden coin and invite students to name the coin you are describing. After the correct coin is named, remove it from the pouch and show the class. Next, invite a child to place a coin in the pouch and give clues to his classmates. As a follow-up, have each youngster make a pouch. Then provide coin manipulatives for students to take home to play the game with a family member.

Feed the Money Muncher

Counting pennies

To make a Money Muncher, decorate a container with a lid, such as a potato chip canister, to look like a hungry creature. Then cut a slit in the lid and set out penny manipulatives. Recite the rhyme, "Money Muncher, Money Muncher, munch, munch, munch. How about [four cents] for your lunch?" At the end of the rhyme, invite a student to feed the Money Muncher a corresponding number of pennies. Then remove the coins and invite the class to verify the coin amount. **To practice recognition of coin names,** insert the name of a coin in the rhyme.

Donna Follett, Kids Inn, Amherst, NH

Penny Pocket   Nickel Pocket

Full Pockets

Exchanging pennies for nickels

This simple center helps students remember that five pennies equal one nickel. To prepare, make a workmat as shown. Also mask the side with six dots on a die and draw one dot in its place. Place the die, the mat, and penny and nickel manipulatives at a center. A child rolls the die and places the same amount of pennies on the penny pocket. Each time she collects five pennies, she trades them for a nickel and places the nickel on the nickel pocket. She continues rolling and trading until she has ten nickels.

adapted from an idea by Misty Strange, Brantly Elementary, Antlers, OR

A Perfect Purchase

Counting coins

To prepare for this small-group game, place in a small resealable plastic bag a different coin amount for each child. Then write on the board each coin amount above a simple illustration of an item. To play, have each child count the coins in his bag and determine which item he has exactly enough money to buy. In turn, invite each student to place his bag on the board ledge under the correct amount. After enlisting students' help in checking the placement of each bag, redistribute the bags and play again.

adapted from an idea by Pam Dunham, Franklin Elementary, Creston, IA

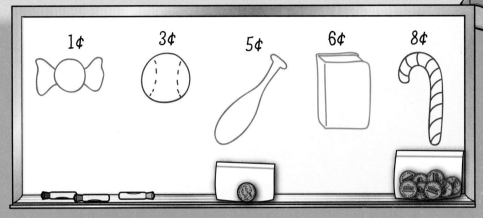

Singing Makes "Cents"!

Recognizing coins

Sing these songs with your kindergartners to help them learn about a penny, a nickel, a dime, and a quarter.

Penny Song
(sung to the tune of "Bingo")

There is a coin that's worth one cent,
And penny is its name, oh!
P-E-N-N-Y, P-E-N-N-Y, P-E-N-N-Y,
And penny is its name, oh!

There is a coin that's brown and round,
And penny is its name, oh!
P-E-N-N-Y, P-E-N-N-Y, P-E-N-N-Y,
And penny is its name, oh!

There is a coin with President Lincoln,
And penny is its name, oh!
P-E-N-N-Y, P-E-N-N-Y, P-E-N-N-Y,
And penny is its name, oh!

Sandy Ryan, Greencastle Elementary,
Silver Spring, MD

Nickel Song
(sung to the tune of "I'm a Little Teapot")
I'm a little nickel,
Can you see?
I've got President
Jefferson on me.
When you go to spend me,
Don't forget
That I am worth
Exactly five cents!

adapted from a song by Sandy Ryan

Quarter Song
(sung to the tune of "Clementine")

Found a quarter, found a quarter,
Found a quarter just now.
Just now I found a quarter,
Found a quarter just now.

It is bigger, it is bigger,
It is bigger than the rest.
It is round and it is silver
And it's worth 25 cents!

Dime Song
(sung to the tune of "Ten Little Indians")

One little, two little, three little pennies,
Four little, five little, six little pennies,
Seven little, eight little, nine little pennies,
Ten pennies equal a dime!

Marjorie Davis, San Diego Independent School
District, San Diego, TX

Coins

Sorting pennies, nickels, dimes, and quarters

Hop to the Shop

Cut.

Glue to match.

Penny 1¢	Nickel 5¢	Dime 10¢	Quarter 25¢

©The Mailbox® • TEC42040 • Dec./Jan. 2008–9

"Purr-fect" Ways to Celebrate the 100th Day!

Comparing Collections

Investigating weight

In advance, give each child a sandwich-size resealable plastic bag to take home. Instruct her to place 100 of the same item in the bag and then return it to school on a designated day. Suggest she select small items, such as paper clips, cereal pieces, pennies, macaroni noodles, or paper squares.

Collect the bags and display two of them. Ask youngsters to predict which bag of items is heavier. Then place each bag on opposite ends of a balance scale and have students check their predictions. Continue with different bags. If desired, place the materials at a center for independent practice.

Hayley Moldenhauer, Our Savior's Lutheran School, Bylas, AZ

A Group Effort

Counting to 100

The result of this class activity is a high-flying display perfect for the 100th day of school! Explain to students that they are going to work together to make 100 balloons. Divide the class into ten groups and tell students that if each group makes ten balloons, there will be 100 balloons in all. Provide each group with a balloon tracer, construction paper, and scissors. Have group members work as a team to make ten balloons. After all the groups have finished, lead students in counting the balloons. Then display the balloons with the title "Up and Away With 100 Days!"

Deanne D'Imperio
Martin Luther King Elementary
Paterson, NJ

Would You Rather...?

Developing oral language

To prepare, program paper strips with different items (see suggestions) and place the strips in a bag. Invite a child to draw two strips and help him read each one. Ask him to tell which item he would rather have and explain why. If desired, write his response on a sheet of chart paper. Then encourage other students to tell why they agree or disagree with the child's response.

I would rather have 100 cupcakes than 100 bees. Cupcakes are good to eat. Bees can sting me and that would hurt.

I would rather have 100 bees than 100 cupcakes because bees make good honey.

Suggestions for Items
100 cupcakes
100 bees
100 dollars
100 markers
100 snakes
100 bananas
100 pizzas
100 buttons
100 dirty socks
100 gumdrops

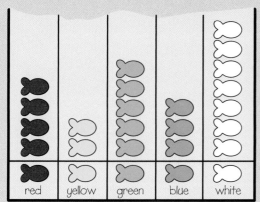

red	yellow	green	blue	white

Super Search

Graphing

Use any die-cut shape and a large sheet of bulletin board paper for this graphing activity. Prepare 100 of the same die-cut shapes in four or five different colors and make a simple graph like the one shown. Scatter the cutouts around the classroom. Before sending students off to collect the cutouts, tell youngsters how many cutouts each child will need to find for the class to find 100 in all. Next, send students (a few at a time) to collect the predetermined number of cutouts. After all the cutouts have been found, ask each youngster to sort her cutouts by color. Then invite each child, in turn, to tape her cutouts to the prepared graph. Lead youngsters to interpret the results of the graph.

Debbie Hill, Stone Elementary, Crossville, TN

All Mixed Up!

Counting by tens, number order

For this whole-group activity, place in a bag the number cards for counting by tens from 10 through 100. Invite ten youngsters to each take a card, identify its number, and stand holding the card so the number faces outward. Then lead the seated students in putting the numbers in order from least to greatest. To check their work, have youngsters count by tens. **For an added challenge,** have nine students each take a card and arrange themselves in order. Then ask the class to determine the missing number.

adapted from an idea by Mairin Jensen
Prairie Elementary
Worthington, MN

Made to Measure

Fuzzy Worms

Using nonstandard units

Youngsters wiggle their way into measurement fun with this idea. To make a supply of worms, cut pipe cleaners into several equal-size pieces. Demonstrate how to measure an object using the worms. Then give each student a few worms and designate an object for him to measure. Have him measure the object and draw a picture to represent the measurement. When each child is finished, invite youngsters to share their drawings.

Briana Wright, New Prospect Elementary, Inman, SC

ALL ABOUT WORMS

Tip: For added fun, use bumpy pipe cleaners.

Gifts Galore

Comparing heights

Let the gift-giving fun begin in your math center. Set out wrapped boxes and gift bags of varying heights. A student chooses two gifts and uses appropriate vocabulary to compare their heights. She repeats this process several times with different gift pairs. Then she orders all the gifts from tallest to shortest.

adapted from an idea by Marie E. Cecchini
West Dundee, IL

How Tall?

Height

Add a seasonal twist to measuring with this partner activity. To make a measuring station, attach seasonal cutouts end to end vertically along a wall to a height taller than the tallest student. Invite a pair of students to the measuring station. Ask one child in the twosome to stand beside the cutouts and have his partner count the cutouts to measure his height. Then direct students to switch roles. Next, help each child write on a sentence strip to describe his height. After all students have completed the activity, post the sentences near the station.

Jamie Topp, W. O. Gray Elementary, Balch Springs, TX

James is about 10 hearts tall.

Nicholas is about 12 hearts tall.

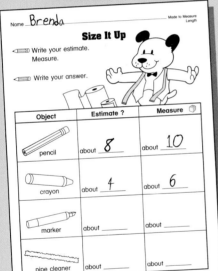

Estimate and Measure

Length

For each student in a small group, put the following objects in a bag: an unsharpened pencil, a pipe cleaner, a new crayon, and a marker. Give each child a bag and a copy of the recording sheet on page 274. Display a Unifix cube for students to use as a measurement reference. Have each child estimate the length of each object in cubes and then use a crayon to record her answer. Next, make more cubes available and direct each student to measure and record the actual length of each object in cubes. After students are finished, invite them to compare their estimates to the actual measurements.

Amy Rodriguez, P. S. 212, Brooklyn, NY

Getting in Step

Comparing objects by length

Use movement to review the concepts of short and long. Gather a ruler and a supply of objects that are shorter and longer than the ruler. Have students stand side by side in an open area. Stand several feet in front of students and show them the ruler alongside one of the objects. Ask youngsters to compare the object to the ruler. If they determine that the object is longer than the ruler, they take a long step toward you. If it is shorter, they take a short step toward you. Continue play with the remaining objects until the class reaches you.

Size It Up

Write your estimate.
Measure.

Write your answer.

Object	Estimate ?	Measure
pencil	about _____	about _____
crayon	about _____	about _____
marker	about _____	about _____
pipe cleaner	about _____	about _____

©The Mailbox® • TEC42041 • Feb./Mar. 2009

Note to the teacher: Use with "Estimate and Measure" on page 273.

MATH Is Just Ducky!

ideas by Ada Goren, Winston-Salem, NC

Flying, Diving, Swimming

Making patterns

With this whole-group activity, youngsters learn about duck behavior. In advance, cut out several copies of the flying, diving, and swimming duck cards on page 277. Explain that some ducks can fly, float on the water, and dive under the water. Then have students help you arrange the ducks to make a pattern. Next, help youngsters say the pattern aloud. Then encourage students to repeat the pattern, adding actions to demonstrate flying, swimming, and diving.

Time to Swim!

Telling time to the hour

Use the swimming duck card on page 277 to make a supply of duck cards. Place the ducks near a pond cutout. To begin, set a timer for three minutes. Then display a time to the hour on a manipulative clock. Have a child name the time and then place a duck on the pond. Continue having students identify times and put ducks in the pond, prompting them to move as fast as possible so they get several ducks in the pond before the timer rings. At a later time, challenge your group to improve its score!

Comparing Quackers

Identifying and comparing numbers

To prepare for this small-group activity, make an even number of swimming duck cards (pattern on page 277). Write a different number on each duck and place the ducks in a pocket chart with the numbers facing to the back. Place a pond cutout nearby. A child turns over two ducks. She names the numbers and identifies which is larger and which is smaller. Then she places the ducks on the pond. Youngsters continue until all the ducks have been placed on the pond.

Ducks on the Lake

Adding with manipulatives

Give each child several yellow pom-poms (ducks) and a sheet of blue paper (lake). Recite the rhyme shown, encouraging youngsters to add the corresponding sets of ducks to their lakes. Then have students count the sets and name the total. Repeat the activity several times, changing the numbers as desired.

There were [five] little ducks on the lake one day.
[Seven] more ducks came to splash and play.
How many ducks were on that lake?
What number does [five] plus [seven] make?

How Colorful!

Data collection, tally chart

Are there more yellow or more white ducks in the pond? That's what students find out during this activity! Cut out a supply of swimming duck cards (pattern on page 277), some from white paper and some from yellow paper. Place the ducks in a bag near a large pond cutout. Also title and label a blank tally chart as shown. Post the chart within students' reach.

To begin the activity, have each child, in turn, take a duck from the bag and draw a tally mark on the chart to show the duck's color. Then have him place the duck on the pond. After each child contributes to the chart, discuss the results with the class.

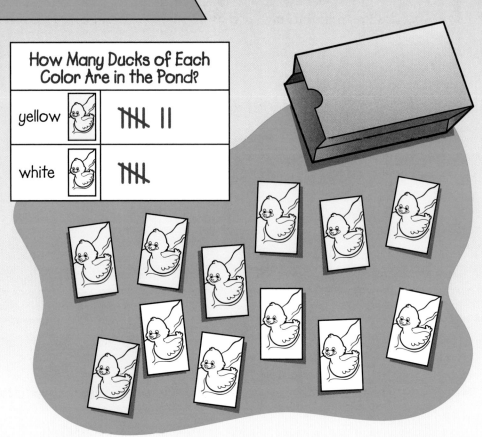

Diving Duck Card
Use with "Flying, Diving, Swimming" on page 275.

Swimming Duck Card
Use with "Flying, Diving, Swimming" and "Time to Swim!" on page 275 and "Comparing Quackers" and "How Colorful!" on page 276.

TEC42042

TEC42042

Flying Duck Card
Use with "Flying, Diving, Swimming" on page 275.

TEC42042

Hands-On Addition

Helpful Plates
Beginning addition

Give each child a three-section animal-shaped plate and a supply of counters. Announce an addition problem and have each student place the matching number of counters in each of the small sections of her plate. Then have her find the sum by combining the counters in the large section of her plate and counting them. **For more advanced students,** have them write each addition problem on a sheet of paper.

Kathleen Stearns
Cherrywood Elementary
San Jose, CA

How Many Candles?
Beginning addition

To prepare for this whole-group activity, cut several paper strips from two different colors of construction paper to make a supply of birthday candles. Then draw a simple birthday cake on the board and place the candles nearby. As you announce a birthday-related story problem, have student volunteers tape the candles to the cake to match the problem. Write the corresponding addition problem on the board. Then lead the class in counting the candles to find the sum.

Marie E. Cecchini
West Dundee, IL

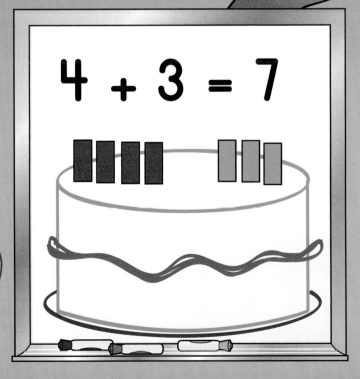

$$4 + 3 = 7$$

The Ten Challenge

Ways to make ten

Small, seasonal erasers make perfect manipulatives! Give each child in a small group ten erasers. Have him arrange the erasers in two groups. Then have him record the corresponding addition sentence on a sheet of paper. He continues in the same manner, creating as many different combinations that equal ten as he can.

Marie E. Cecchini
West Dundee, IL

Roll, Add, and Color

Addition to 12

For this partner game, give each child a copy of page 280 and give each twosome a pair of dice. In turn, each youngster rolls the dice and adds the numbers. On her paper she colors a space programmed with the corresponding sum. If the number is already colored, her turn is over. Play continues until both students have revealed the hidden picture.

Beth Fondale
St. Rose Catholic School
New Lexington, OH

Musical Math

Writing addition sentences

Kindergartners tune up their adding skills with this rhythmic idea. Use a musical instrument such as a tambourine and have students count each note you play. Then have each child write the number of notes on a sheet of paper. Repeat the process using a different instrument such as a drum. Finally, have each youngster add the numbers together and record the sum.

Kelsea Wright
Seal Elemenatry
Douglass, KS

1, 2, 3, 4...

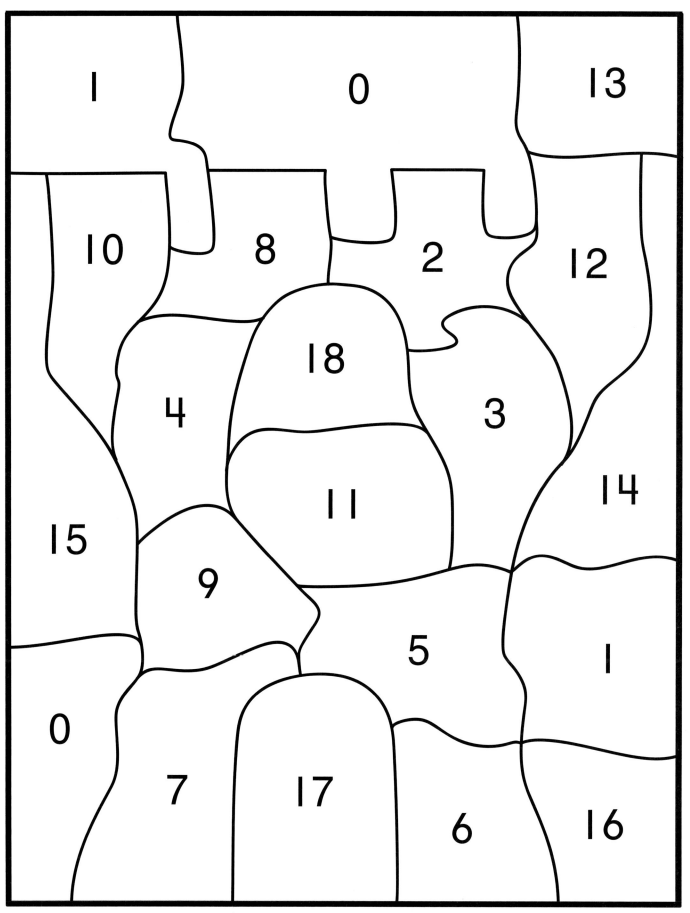

©The Mailbox® • TEC42043 • June/July 2009

280 THE MAILBOX   **Note to the teacher:** Use with "Roll, Add, and Color" on page 279.

SEASONAL UNITS

Terrific Tools
for Back-to-School

Welcome! Welcome!
Song

Help youngsters warm up to the new school year with this catchy tune! Teach students the song. Then post a different verse on each of three days and have students circle a designated high-frequency word—such as *at, and,* or *the*—each time it appears.

(sung to the tune of "London Bridge")

All the children are at school,
Are at school, are at school.
All the children are at school.
Welcome! Welcome!

Books and pencils, teachers and friends,
Teachers and friends, teachers and friends.
Books and pencils, teachers and friends.
It's time for learning!

This school year will be the best,
Be the best, be the best.
This school year will be the best.
We're so happy!

adapted from an idea by Julie Granchelli
W. P. Towne Elementary
Medina, NY

Treasured Sights
School tour

For this first-day activity, bring in a toy treasure chest and gather several small treasures, such as shiny beads, imitation gold coins, and seashells. Put a note with the message shown in the empty chest. Hide a treasure at each school location with which you would like students to become familiar.

To begin, direct students' attention to the treasure chest and read the note with mock surprise. Then take students on a school tour, stopping at each chosen location for youngsters to find and collect the hidden treasure. After you return to your classroom, have students recall the locations they visited as they put the treasures in the chest.

Sandra Bonny, West Irvine Elementary, Irvine, KY

Tour the school with a watchful eye
And the treasures you will spy.

Who's Who?
Class book

Reinforce concepts about print as you familiarize students with school staff members. Here's how! Collect an individual photo of yourself and of each staff member with whom students will interact regularly. Mount each photo on a separate copy of the booklet page from page 284. After students have met each staff member, complete each page as shown with students' input. Bind the completed pages between two covers and title the resulting book "School Workers, School Workers." When you read the book with students, point to each word, in turn, and encourage youngsters to chime in.

Elizabeth Newmark, Brick Mill Elementary
Middletown, DE

Ms. Stevens , Ms. Stevens ,
what do you do?

I ___teach music___
at our wonderful school.

A Perfect Fit
Display

This name idea results in eye-catching projects that are ideal for an open house display. For each child, copy the puzzle pieces from page 285 so there is one piece for each letter in his first name plus one more. Write his name on the puzzle pieces, positioning the pieces so the dots are at the bottom. Have him color the pieces, cut them out, and glue a small photo of himself on the blank piece. Then ask him to glue the pieces on a strip of black paper so the lettered pieces spell his name and the piece with the photo is last. Display students' completed puzzles with the title "We All Fit Together!"

Tammy Willey, Pine Street Elementary, Presque Isle, ME

Special Someone
Group activity

To help youngsters get acquainted, sit with them in a circle. Secretly choose one youngster and sing the song below. Then give students a clue to the youngster's identity, such as "She is wearing pink." Once students successfully identify the youngster, ask her to stand. Then lead the class in greeting her by name. After she sits back down, secretly choose another student and sing the song again. Continue as described until the group has greeted each youngster.

(sung to the tune of "Mary Had a Little Lamb")

I am thinking of someone,
Of someone, of someone.
I am thinking of someone.
It's someone in this class.

Lucille Iscaro, P. S. 257, Bronx, NY

That's me!

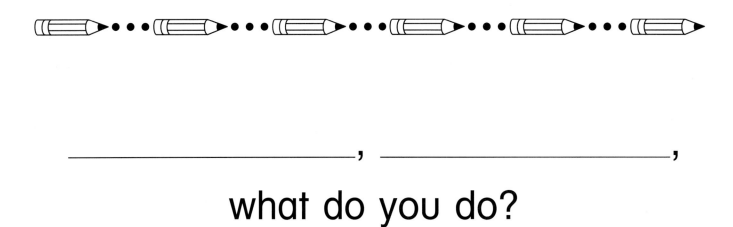

_____, _____,

what do you do?

I _____

at our wonderful school.

Note to the teacher: Use with "Who's Who?" on page 283.

Puzzle Patterns
Use with "A Perfect Fit" on page 283.

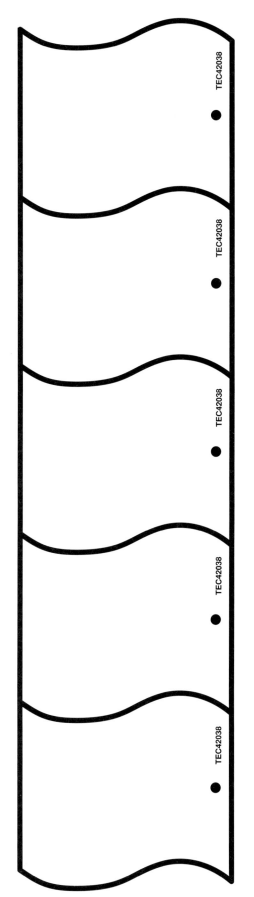

School Notes
Use copies of the notes below as desired
to brighten each student's day.

_____,

I'm tickled pink you're here today!

_____
teacher

_____
date

had a sunshiny day!

_____   _____
teacher   date

THE MAILBOX **285**

Seasonal Skill Practice
Apples

Wormy Surprise

To make this adorable booklet, instruct each child to color, cut out, and sequence a copy of the booklet pages from page 288. Then fold a 4" x 10" paper strip in half and staple the pages inside. Ask the youngster to add his name and an illustration to the booklet cover. Next, give him a narrow four-inch green rectangle that you have trimmed to make a worm. Instruct him to draw a face on one end of the worm. Punch a hole in the opposite end and tie a 12-inch string through it. Tape the free end of the string inside the booklet on the back cover. Then reinforce skills as described below.

Print awareness: As you read the booklet with students, have them track the print with their worms.

Rhyming: Ask students to identify the rhyming words.

Word recognition: Instruct each youngster to highlight the word *apple* each time it appears. Or have him use different-colored crayons to underline high-frequency words such as *a, an, has,* and *is.*

adapted from an idea by Laura Wanke, Pecatonica Elementary, Pecatonica, IL

Toss and Pick!

When it comes to being easy to adapt, these floor mat activities are the pick of the crop! Place a large tree cutout on the floor. Make a class supply of apple cutouts and choose an option below. (If the tree is too small to hold all the apples, set some apples aside and restock the tree after students "pick" several apples.)

Student names or high-frequency words: Program the apples with students' names or high-frequency words, writing one word per apple. Place the apples word side down on the tree. Invite each student, in turn, to toss a beanbag on the tree and then "pick" the apple nearest the beanbag. Ask the group to read the corresponding word and spell it aloud.

Number sense: Write a number on each apple (you may repeat numbers). Put the apples on the tree number side down. Have each youngster, in turn, toss a beanbag on the tree and then "pick" the apple nearest the beanbag. Instruct her to read the number on the apple and lead the group in clapping the corresponding number of times.

Kathryn Davenport, Partin Elementary, Oviedo, FL

From Seed to Tree

Use this catchy song to teach students that apple trees come from seeds. After youngsters are familiar with the lyrics, have them recall from the song what the seeds need to grow. Explain that in addition to soil and water, the seeds also need air and sunlight. ***Understanding how plants grow***

(sung to the tune of "Sing a Song of Sixpence")

I took a little apple seed
And put it in the ground.
I filled the hole with soil
And poured water around.
The little seed soon sprouted;
It grew into a tree.
Now it has big red apples
Just right for you and me!

Deborah Garmon, Groton, CT

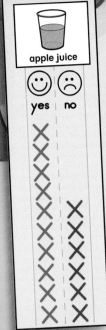

That's Tasty!

For this taste test, make a class supply of the recording sheet on page 289 plus one extra. Cut from one copy the illustrated boxes in the first column. Then glue each box at the top of a separate vertical sentence strip. Add simple face illustrations and labels as shown. To begin, arrange for each youngster to sample the foods listed on the recording sheet. Have him color the appropriate faces on his recording sheet. Then compile students' responses on the sentence strips as shown to make simplified graphs. Guide youngsters to compare the results. ***Completing a chart, graphing***

Jennie Cashman
Bennett Elementary
Bennett, IA

What's Inside?

Do big apples have more seeds than small apples? That's one of several questions students may explore with this guess-and-check activity. Arrange three different apples in a row. Illustrate and label a separate blank card for each apple and then display the cards near the apples.

Have students predict how many seeds the first apple contains. Then cut the apple, count the seeds, and write the corresponding number on the appropriate card. Next, ask students to predict how many seeds the second apple contains. After you check the predictions as described, write the actual number of seeds on the matching card. Repeat the predicting, checking, and recording process with the third apple. Students may be surprised to learn that regardless of size, color, or variety, most apples have five to ten seeds! ***Making predictions***

Marie E. Cecchini, West Dundee, IL

I think the small apple has four seeds.

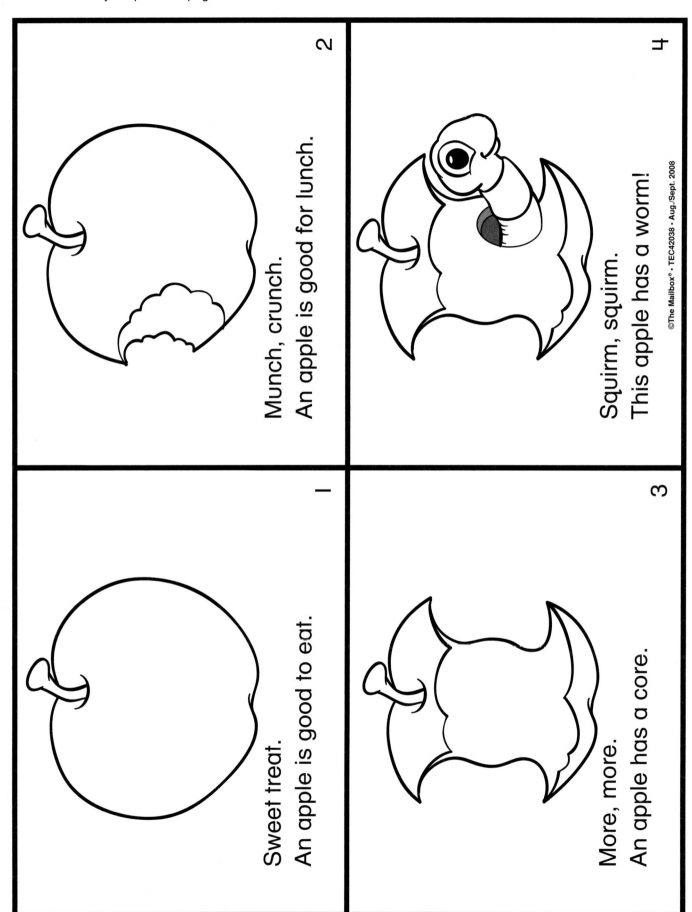

2

Munch, crunch.
An apple is good for lunch.

4

Squirm, squirm.
This apple has a worm!

©The Mailbox® • TEC42038 • Aug./Sept. 2008

1

Sweet treat.
An apple is good to eat.

3

More, more.
An apple has a core.

Taste Test

Follow your teacher's directions.

What I Tasted	Did I Like It?	
 **apple juice**	😊 yes	😞 no
apple jelly	😊 yes	😞 no
apple cereal	😊 yes	😞 no
applesauce	😊 yes	😞 no

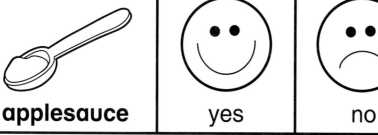

Note to the teacher: Use with "That's Tasty!" on page 287.

Constitution Day

Reasons for Rules

What better way to introduce the topic of the U.S. Constitution than by discussing the importance of rules? Review with students why each of your classroom rules is important. Then ask students to imagine what a grocery store, a bank, and other locations in the community would be like without rules. After students share their ideas, point out that rules are important everywhere to help people get along and stay safe. Then show students a picture of the Constitution and explain that it contains rules, or laws, for the United States.

Freedom, Rights, and Laws

Post on chart paper the poem shown. Read the poem with students and choose from the ideas below.

Phonological awareness: Circle the word *Constitution.* Clap once for each syllable as you say the word and have students count the syllables. Then invite students to clap as they repeat the word with you.

Vocabulary: Discuss with students what the words *freedom, rights,* and *laws* mean to them.

Social studies: Give each student a paper with a sentence starter such as "I am glad our country has laws because…" Help him complete the sentence and have him illustrate his work.

Word recognition: Write each of the following words on separate blank cards: *freedom, rights,* and *laws.* Have students find the matching words in the poem and underline them.

High-frequency words: Give each student a copy of the poem. Have her highlight words such as *and, it, the,* and *we.*

The Constitution was written long ago;
We honor it today.
It gives Americans freedom and rights
And laws that lead the way.

Seasonal Skill Practice
Leaves

ideas contributed by Ada Goren
Winston-Salem, NC

Colorful Favorites

Use this idea over a few days for different skills! To prepare, write on sentence strips the poem shown, drawing blanks in place of the color words. Display the poem in a pocket chart, adding the color words on separate sentence strips. For each color word, put a matching leaf card (patterns on page 293) in the corresponding pocket. To begin, read the poem with students a few times. Next, invite student volunteers to rearrange the color words and change the leaf cards to match. Then ask students to read the revised poem. Follow up with the ideas below.

Letter recognition: Have students find the words that begin with the letter *l*.

Color words: Display the poem without the leaves. Make a second set of color word cards, writing the words with markers of the corresponding colors. Have students read the cards and place them on the matching words in the poem.

High-frequency words: Frame chosen words and ask students to read them.

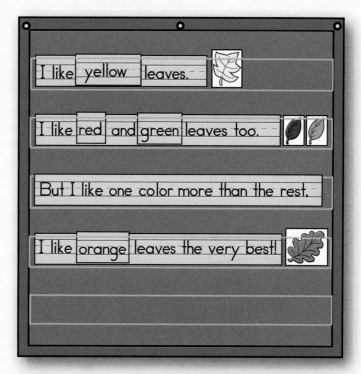

I like yellow leaves.

I like red and green leaves too.

But I like one color more than the rest,

I like orange leaves the very best!

Paired to Compare!

Begin this observation activity by taking your students on a walk outdoors. Have each young-ster collect a leaf that has fallen to the ground before he returns to the classroom. (Or give each child a colorful copy of a leaf card from page 293, ensuring that there is a variety of leaves among students.) Next, pair students and give each youngster a copy of the recording sheet from page 294. Have each child write his name and his part-ner's name where indicated. Ask him to illustrate their leaves in the corresponding boxes and circle the appropriate words to describe the leaves. Then guide him to write how the leaves are alike and different. ***Observing similarities and differences***

Fluttering Free

For this hands-on approach to subtraction, draw a large tree on a whiteboard. Use loops of tape to loosely attach to the tree a chosen number of oak leaf cards. (See the patterns at the bottom of page 293). To begin, say the poem shown, pausing after the second line to remove the appropriate number of cards. At the end of the poem, have students determine how many leaves remain on the tree. Model different subtraction problems in the same manner. **For more advanced students,** after you model a problem, have each youngster write the corresponding subtraction sentence on an individual whiteboard. *Beginning subtraction*

[Eight] pretty leaves on the old oak tree.
[Two] pretty leaves flutter free.
How many leaves do you still see
Up in the branches of the old oak tree?

Two-Sided Tree

This art project is a great avenue for explaining why leaves change colors in the fall! Give each youngster a large white tree cutout like the one shown. Instruct her to use a brown marker to color the tree trunk and draw branches. Then have her use green paint to make handprints or sponge prints on the treetop.

After the paint dries, tell students that the chlorophyll in a tree's leaves helps make food for the tree and makes the leaves green. Explain that as the tree gets ready to rest for the winter, the chlorophyll fades away. Guide students to realize that the green color disappears as this happens. Explain that the leaves then show colors (red, orange, and yellow) that the green color had hidden. Next, have each youngster color the trunk and draw branches on the blank side of her tree. Then ask her to make fall-colored paint prints on the treetop. The result will be a handy reminder of what she learned about leaves! *Understanding seasonal changes of leaves*

Leaf Cards

Use with "Colorful Favorites" and "Paired to Compare!" on page 291.

TEC42039

TEC42039

TEC42039

TEC42039

TEC42039

TEC42039

TEC42039

Oak Leaf Cards

Use with "Colorful Favorites" and "Paired to Compare!" on page 291 and "Fluttering Free" on page 292.

TEC42039

TEC42039

My Name:

_____

My Leaf

Size: ○ small   ○ medium   ○ large

Edges: 〜 jagged   ⌒ smooth

My Partner's Name:

_____

My Partner's Leaf

Size: ○ small   ○ medium   ○ large

Edges: 〜 jagged   ⌒ smooth

Same: _____

Different: _____

©The Mailbox® • TEC42039 • Oct./Nov. 2008

294 THE MAILBOX   **Note to the teacher:** Use with "Paired to Compare!" on page 291.

Colonial Kids

ideas contributed by Laurie K. Gibbons
Huntsville, AL

Different and Alike
Identifying similarities and differences

As you teach students this song, guide them to compare their lives with the lives of colonial children.

(sung to the first verse of "My Bonnie Lies Over the Ocean")

Colonial children were different
From the children today, we know.
They worked hard from sunup to sundown
And rarely to school could they go.

Colonial children did chores then
To help with their families' needs.
They cooked and they gardened and hunted
And did different household deeds.

Colonial children were also
Like so many children today.
They laughed and learned and they had great fun
With the games they liked to play!

Peek at the Past
Developing vocabulary

This cabin project holds reminders of how colonial children spent their time! Have each child place a copy of the cabin pattern from page 296 on a piece of corrugated paper and then do a crayon rubbing on it. After he adds any other desired crayon details, staple the top of the house to a blank sheet of paper. Then have the youngster cut out the house through both thicknesses. Next, ask the youngster to open the resulting booklet and glue an envelope facedown on the back cover, keeping the flap free. Then instruct him to color and cut out a copy of the picture cards from page 297 and store them in the envelope. Follow up with the ideas below.

Action words: Read the cards' captions with students. Then have students underline the action words and act them out.

Categorizing: Help students sort the cards by the categories of work, play, and school. (*Work: sampler, butter churn, and chickens; Play: hoop, top, and kite; School: hornbook and feather quill*)

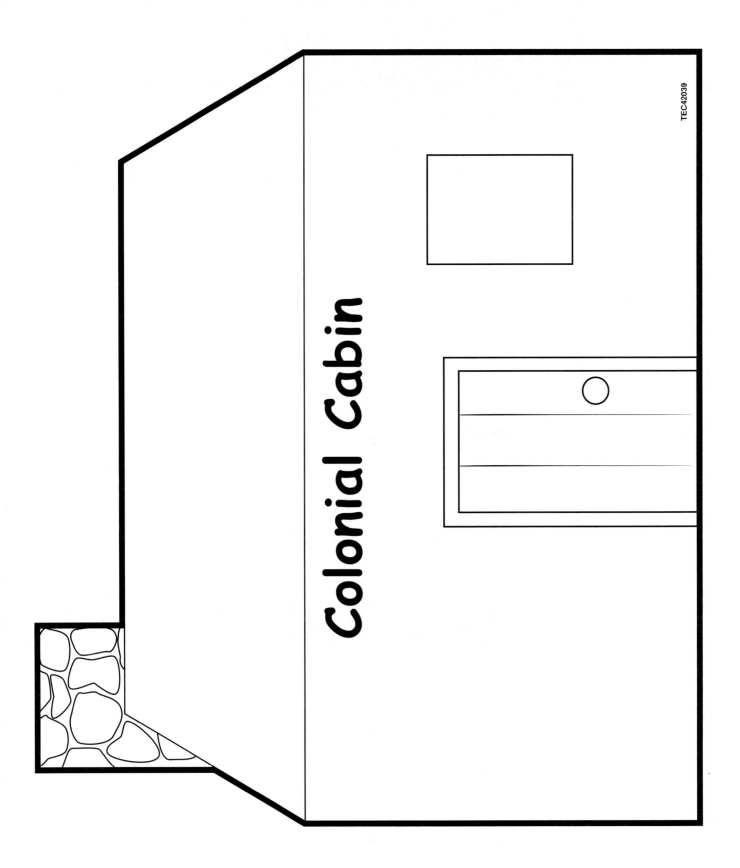

Colonial Cabin

TEC42039

Read a hornbook.

TEC42039

Sew a sampler.

TEC42039

Roll a hoop with a stick.

TEC42039

Churn some butter.

TEC42039

Feed the chickens.

TEC42039

Spin a top.

TEC42039

Write with a feather quill.

TEC42039

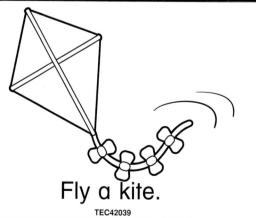

Fly a kite.

TEC42039

Bear Booklet

This booklet-making project is the perfect complement to Bill Martin Jr.'s books *Brown Bear, Brown Bear, What Do You See?* and *Polar Bear, Polar Bear, What Do You Hear?* After reading aloud the books, explain that authors often use their five senses to imagine what it would be like to be a character in a book. Next, share some basic facts about polar bears and brown bears. Then ask each child to imagine that he is either a polar bear or a brown bear. Use the directions below to help each child make a bear booklet. Have him complete the sentence on each booklet page by drawing, writing, or dictating a response. ***Completing sentences***

Steps to make one bear booklet:
1. Choose to make a polar bear or a brown bear. Make a cover by decorating a white (polar bear) or a brown (brown bear) seven-inch paper oval to look like a bear head. If desired, cut ears from construction paper scraps and glue them to the head.
2. Cut six seven-inch ovals (booklet pages) from blank paper.
3. Glue each sentence strip from a copy of the top of page 300 to a separate booklet page.
4. Staple the pages in order behind the cover.

Laurie K. Gibbons, Huntsville, AL

Bearing the Cold

Model how a polar bear keeps warm in cold arctic weather with this simple investigation. Label one resealable plastic bag "A" and another "B." Partially fill bag A with shortening and tape it shut. Remove all the air from bag B, seal it, and tape it shut. To begin the investigation, place several ice cubes on a plate. Ask students to tell how ice feels when it is touched. Then show them both bags. Invite each child to predict which bag will make the ice feel less cold when placed between her hand and the ice. Next, have each student take a turn touching the ice with each bag. Lead the class to determine that the ice does not feel as cold when bag A is used. Then explain that the shortening in the bag is like the layer of blubber, or fat, under a polar bear's skin, which helps it survive in the cold. ***Animal adaptations***

Laurie K. Gibbons

Bear Hunt

Baby bears, baby bears,
Where could you be?
If you rhyme with [hat],
Please come to me!

For this whole-group activity, cut out a copy of the big bear cards on page 301 and enough copies of the baby bear cards for each child to have one. Tape each big bear card to a crepe paper necklace. To begin, invite a child to be the big bear and wear a necklace. Give each remaining youngster a baby bear card. Help the big bear recite the verse shown, inserting the word from his necklace. At the end of the verse, ask each student with a rhyming word card to join the big bear. After reviewing the rhymes, redistribute the baby bear cards and invite another student to wear a different big bear necklace. **Rhyming**

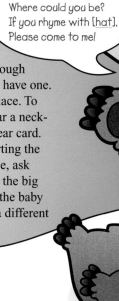

I wld et

WRITING

A Beastly Feast

Explain that some bears eat a large amount of food before settling in for a long winter's rest. Then give each child two paper cave cutouts, one brown and one white. Direct her to write about and draw on the white paper different foods she would like to eat if she were a bear getting ready for her winter rest. Then have her draw on the brown paper herself as a bear. Help each child staple the brown cave cutout atop the white paper. **Responding to a prompt**

All Lined Up

CENTERS

MATH: Make five copies of the bear card on page 300. Color each one a different color. Set out the bears and copies of the bear strip and task cards from page 300. A student lines up the bears as desired and colors a strip to match. Then she completes a task card and glues the card and strip to a sheet of paper. **Ordinal numbers**

1st

Name Carolyn
Color to show where each 🐻 is in line.

3rd   2nd
1st   5th
4th

LITERACY: Set out brown paper circles and uppercase letter cards. A child adds details to two circles so they resemble bear paw prints. Next, he names the letter on a card and writes it on one paw print. He writes the lowercase form of the letter on the other print. Then he glues the prints on a strip of construction paper as shown. He continues with other letters. **Uppercase and lowercase letters**

Laurie K. Gibbons, Huntsville, AL

Sentence Strips

Use with "Bear Booklet" on page 298.

1 If I were a _____ bear,	**2** 👁 I would see
3 👃 I would smell	**4** 👂 I would hear
5 🐾 I would feel	**6** 👄 I would taste

Bear Strip, Bear Card, and Task Card

Use with "All Lined Up" on page 299.

1st

TEC42040

Name _____

🖍 Color to show where each 🐻 is in line.

🐻 3rd   🐻 2nd

🐻 1st   🐻 5th

🐻 4th

TEC42040

hat

log

sock

TEC42040

cat

dog

rock

TEC42040

rat

frog

clock

TEC42040

bat

jog

lock

TEC42040

Seasonal Skill Practice
♥ ♥ ♥ Valentine's Day ♥ ♥ ♥

MATH
Valentine Mail

To prepare, draw lines to divide a sheet of paper into 12 sections. Draw a heart in each section to make valentine cards; then label each card with a different number word, color word, or shape word. Give each child a copy of the paper and three envelopes. Help him label each envelope as shown. After he cuts out the cards, instruct him to sort each card into the correct envelope. **For an added challenge,** have each student draw or color on the back of each card to match the word. *Classification*

adapted from an idea by Nikki Buwalda
Randolph Elementary
Randolph, WI

Number Words

Color Words

Shape Words

LITERACY
Find It, Read It!

Reuse valentine cards with this simple center. On a sheet of poster board, glue several valentine cards that contain high-frequency words; then laminate the poster. Make a list of the high-frequency words. Place the list, the poster, and dry-erase markers at a center. A child reads each word on the list and then uses the marker to circle it each time it is found on the poster. *High-frequency words*

be

my

will

you

I

to

Susan Keaffaber
O. J. Neighbours Elementary
Wabash, IN

Lovely Times

For this small-group game, cut out a tagboard copy of the pattern on page 304. Make a spinner by attaching a paper clip to the cutout with a brad. Give each child in the group a copy of page 305. To play, a student spins the spinner and reads the time. (If the spinner lands between numbers, the child moves the spinner to the closest number.) Then she finds the matching time on her paper and writes it below the clock. Students take turns until each child has completed her paper. If a player spins a time that is already on her paper, she spins again. ***Time to the hour***

Diane L. Flohr-Henderson
Kent City Elementary
Kent City, MI

Heart Hunt

Program a class supply of heart cutouts with different letters. When the students are out of the classroom, place the hearts around the room. After students return, invite each child to find one heart and then sit down. Ask five students to stand up. Have those youngsters work together to put the letters in alphabetical order. Invite the remaining students to verify the order. Then repeat the activity with five different students. ***Alphabetical order***

Twenty-two?

In the Cup

Give skill practice a fun twist with this class guessing game. Program disposable cups with numbers, letters, words, shapes, or any other skill you would like to reinforce. Choose three cups; then secretly place a small heart cutout or candy heart in one of the cups. Place the cups in a row with the programming facing toward students. Scramble the cups in front of youngsters. Next, ask a volunteer to guess which cup has the heart by reading or naming what is on the cup. Then empty the contents of the cup. After the heart is found, play again with three different cups. ***Skill practice***

Diane L. Flohr-Henderson

TEC42041

Lovely Times

:

:

:

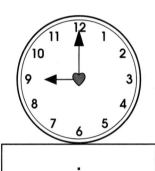

:

:

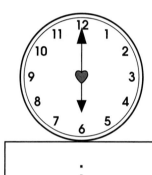

:

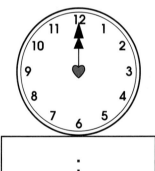

:

:

:

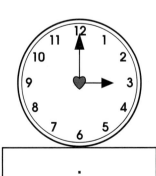

:

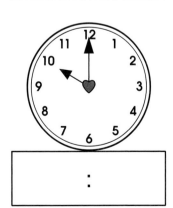

:

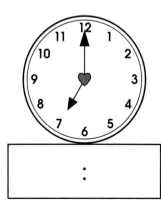

:

Seasonal Skill Practice
Frogs

LITERACY OR MATH
Hop to It!

This easy-to-make gameboard can be used again and again! On a blue piece of poster board (pond), designate an area to start and an area to finish. Next, attach small lily pad cutouts to the board to form a path. Program a couple of lily pads with either "Hop forward" or "Hop back" and include a specific number of spaces. Then cover the board with clear Con-Tact covering for durability. Use the board with the games below.

High-frequency words: Set out word cards and a game marker for each player. To play, a child reads a word aloud. If correct, he counts the number of letters in the word and moves his marker forward the same number of spaces. If incorrect, he asks for help and then reads the word aloud three times before moving forward one space. Reshuffle the cards as needed.

Addition: Set out a pair of dice and a game marker for each player. A child rolls the dice, adds the numbers rolled, and names the sum. To check her work, she counts the total number of dots on the dice. If correct, she rolls one die and moves forward the same number of spaces. If incorrect, her turn ends.

Laurel Rancitelli
St. Joan of Arc-St. George School
Chicopee, MA

Tip: For extra durability, use an old gameboard rather than poster board. Simply cover the board with blue Con-Tact covering.

SCIENCE
From Tadpole to Frog

Use sticky dots for a unique frog life cycle booklet! Help each child accordion-fold a 3" x 18" paper strip to make six sections. In the far left section, help her write the title shown, and in each remaining section have her attach a sticky dot. Then direct the student to add details to each dot, in order, to represent the stages of the frog's life cycle. To complete the booklet, help her label each drawing. **For an easier version,** prepare word strips for each youngster to use to label her drawings. *Life cycle of a frog*

adapted from an idea by Diane Bonica, Deer Creek Elementary, Tigard, OR

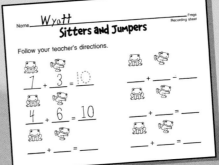

MATH
Sitters and Jumpers

For this addition center, cut out ten copies of the frog card on page 308. Fold each card in half and glue it together so the frogs face out. Store the cards in a bag and place the bag and copies of the recording sheet on page 308 at a center.

To begin, a youngster shakes the bag, empties the contents, and sorts the frogs into two categories: frogs that are sitting and frogs that are jumping. Then he writes the corresponding addition sentence on a recording sheet and solves it. He puts the cards back in the bag and repeats the process until he has completed his paper. ***Beginning addition***

Tracy Combs, Struble Elementary, Cincinnati, OH

Name: **Wyatt**
Frogs
Recording sheet
Sitters and Jumpers
Follow your teacher's directions.

$1 + 3 = 10$

$4 + 6 = 10$

j u m p
jump

LITERACY
Ribbit, Croak, Hop!

To prepare for this center, brainstorm with youngsters a list of frog-themed vocabulary words. Write each word on an individual brown paper strip (log). For each word on a log, write each letter on a green paper square (frog). Place the frogs and logs at a center. A child spells each word by placing the corresponding frogs on each log. **For more advanced students,** have each youngster write the words on another sheet of paper. ***Spelling, building vocabulary***

adapted from an idea by LeeAnn Collins
Sunshine House Preschool
Lansing, MI

I can jump 20 times my length!

MATH
Little Leapers!

Compare your students' jumping abilities to a frog's jump! To illustrate that a frog can jump 20 times its length, line up and tape on the floor 20 frog cutouts (pattern on page 308) numbered from 1 to 20. Use masking tape to mark a starting line by the first frog. Then invite each youngster, in turn, to stand behind the starting line and jump. Have him write the number of frog lengths he jumped and his name on a sticky note. After each child has had a turn, help him stick his paper on a labeled grid to form a graph. Lead youngsters to compare the results. ***Collecting data, graphing***

LeeAnn Collins

Frog Card
Use with "Sitters and Jumpers" on page 307.

Frog Pattern
Use with "Little Leapers" on page 307.

TEC42042

Name_____

Sitters and Jumpers

Follow your teacher's directions.

_____ + _____ = 10   _____ + _____ = _____

_____ + _____ = _____   _____ + _____ = _____

_____ + _____ = _____   _____ + _____ = _____

Note to the teacher: Use the recording sheet with "Sitters and Jumpers" on page 307.

Seasonal Skill Practice
Bugs

ideas contributed by Laurie K. Gibbons, Huntsville, AL

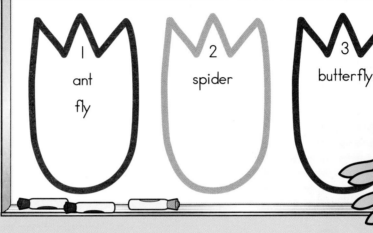

LITERACY
Finding Flowers

Youngsters pretend to be butterflies during this whole-group activity. In advance, draw three flowers on the board and number them. To begin, announce a word that has one, two, or three syllables. Lead students to repeat the word as they "flap their wings" like butterflies once for each word part. Then write the word on the flower that corresponds with the number of word parts. Continue as time allows. **For a more advanced version,** have students segment words into individual sounds using appropriately numbered flower drawings. ***Phonological awareness***

SCIENCE
Build a Bug

Reinforce the parts of a bug with a small-group game. Add a brad and a paper clip to a tagboard copy of the spinner on page 311 as shown. Give each child in the group a copy of the game mat on page 311. In turn, each youngster spins the spinner, identifies the body part, and colors a matching part on his game mat. If the body part is already colored, his turn is over. Play continues until one student has all the body parts colored. ***Parts of an insect***

Made by Bees!

Bees are the inspiration for this measurement activity. In advance, collect a variety of products that are made by bees or can be made from beeswax, such as honey, candles, crayons, shoe polish, or lipstick. Also cut yellow pipe cleaners into one-inch pieces to make a supply of bees. Have students use the bees to measure the lengths of the different items. Then ask each child to choose two items and compare the lengths. **For more advanced students,** have them write and draw to show how two items compare to each other. *Nonstandard measurement*

Bug Jars

For this center activity, cut from construction paper several jar shapes and a supply of ladybugs. Then program the jars and bugs as described in an option below.

Addition: Program each of three jars with a different sum. Then label each ladybug with an addition problem and matching dot sets. A child solves the problem on each ladybug and places the ladybug on the jar with the matching sum.

Number words: Program each of ten jars with a different number word. Then label the ladybugs with the numerals 1–10. A student places each ladybug on the jar with the matching number word.

Letters: Draw a happy face on one jar and a sad face on another. Then label each ladybug with an uppercase and lowercase letter, making sure that some are matching pairs and some are not. A child places correct letter pairs on the happy face and incorrect ones on the sad face. **For an added challenge,** he rewrites each incorrect pair to make it correct.

Busy Bugs

This writing activity doubles as a unique display! Enlist students' help in compiling a list of bug-themed action words. On a white paper strip, have each child write and illustrate a sentence about a bug using one of the listed words. Next, have her glue her strip to the center of a slightly larger piece of black construction paper. After each child has completed her project, punch holes along the top and bottom of each paper. Display the papers in rows to look like a film strip and add the title shown.
Action words

Lights, Camera, Action... Bugs on the Move!

Ants can march.

Fireflies can fly.

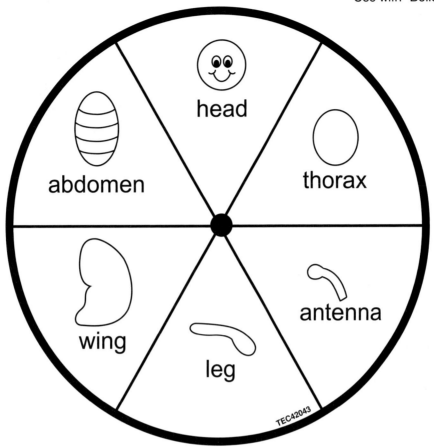

TEC42043

Name_____ Game mat

Build a Bug

Marching Ants

✂ Cut out the 🐜🐜🐜🐜🐜🐜🐜🐜 .

Measure.

_____ ants

_____ ants

_____ ant

_____ ants

_____ ants

INDEX

ISBN-13: 978-156234921-9
ISBN-10: 156234921-X